Towards
a *Moving*
School

Educational Leadership Dialogues

1   *Towards a Moving School*, John Fleming and Elizabeth Kleinhenz
    978-086431-702-5

2   *Learning for Leadership*, Christine Cawsey and Michelle Anderson
    978-086431-631-8

Towards a *Moving* School

Developing a professional learning and performance culture

John Fleming & Elizabeth Kleinhenz

First published 2007
by ACER Press, an imprint of
Australian Council *for* Educational Research Ltd
19 Prospect Hill Road, Camberwell, Victoria 3124

www.acerpress.com.au
sales@acerpress.edu.au

Edited by Susan Keogh
Cover design by Alice Graphics
Text design by Kerry Cooke, eggplant communications
Typeset by Kerry Cooke, eggplant communications
Printed in Australia by BPA Print Group

National Library of Australia Cataloguing-in-Publication data:

Kleinhenz, Elizabeth.
    Towards a moving school : developing a professional learning and
    performance culture.

    Bibliography.
    Includes index.
    ISBN 9780864317025 (pbk.).

    1. Teaching - Australia - Evaluation. 2. Teaching - Australia - Quality control.
    3. Professional education - Australia. 4. Teacher effectiveness - Australia -
    Evaluation. 5. Teacher effectiveness - Australia - Quality control. I. Fleming,
    John (John William), 1955- . II. Australian Council *for* Educational Research.
    III. Title. (Series : Educational leadership dialogues).

371.1440994

The publisher and authors acknowledge the Performance and Development
Culture program of the Victorian Department of Education and Early Childhood
Development and the assistance of the Department, The Boston Consulting Group
and Haileybury College in the preparation of this book.

Foreword

Extensive research has revealed the key role played by the individual teacher in the achievement of student outcomes. However, contemporary research into quality teaching, teacher learning and educational change has also revealed the importance of learning communities and educational leadership in creating cultures in which students and teachers can learn, teachers can teach, and schools can improve (Dinham, 2007a).

Building professional collaboration and accountability among teachers has been found to be effective in promoting teacher professional development and in enhancing educational outcomes for students (Watson & Steele 2006).

Voulalas and Sharpe (2005) note that the concept of the school as a learning community, while universally accepted as desirable, is still vague and ambiguous. This lack of clarity can make attempts to develop learning communities and professional learning cultures in education and elsewhere problematic. A weakness is the failure to address the 'how' aspects of establishing and maintaining learning communities.

Voulalas and Sharpe (2005 p. 191) found that:

> When all the definitions were pieced together the school as a learning community was perceived as a place where life-long learning takes place for all stakeholders for their own continuous growth and development, teachers act as exemplary learners, students are prepared adequately for the future, and mistakes become agents for further learning and improvement. Furthermore, it is a place where collaboration and mutual support is nurtured, clear shared visions for the future are built, and the physical environment contributes to learning.

However, as noted, while defining and describing the learning community is relatively simple, operationalising the concept can be challenging.

In this age, we have grown accustomed to demanding quick fixes and technological solutions to problems—what could be termed the '24-hour help desk mentality'. However, learning communities cannot be mandated, built or operated in a technical, mechanistic sense. Rather, these need to be encouraged, nourished and sustained in the manner of an organic system.

Building a professional learning culture is more like agriculture or gardening than engineering or chemistry. While agriculture is underpinned by both engineering and chemistry, it is a far more inexact and varied undertaking, heavily dependent on the local and wider environment and reliant on knowledge, learning and judgement.

Educational leaders cannot, nor should they attempt to, mandate or force the development of learning communities. As Andy Hargreaves has noted (1994), collegiality cannot be contrived. Leaders can, however, assist staff to come together, focus, learn and collaborate on issues of importance.

Educational leaders also need to ensure that teaching and learning are central concerns of the school and do all in their power to ensure that nothing is allowed to obstruct or distort this central focus (Dinham, 2005).

ACER Press has brought together two highly experienced educators who each shine a light on the phenomenon of the professional learning culture. Dr Elizabeth Kleinhenz from ACER provides a concise yet comprehensive research foundation to the field, while John Fleming, an experienced principal, provides a first-hand account of building a professional learning culture for school improvement. Each highlights the importance of educational leadership that is highly responsive to student and teacher needs, yet is also demanding, incorporating clear, high, agreed standards consistently applied across the school (Dinham, 2007b).

This book makes a valuable contribution to bridging the gap between educational theory and practice and provides a rich and authentic account of how a professional learning culture can be developed to lift student, teacher and school performance. The research and contextualised frameworks provide educators with a clear understanding of the conditions, strategies, processes and challenges underpinning school improvement.

Professor Stephen Dinham, PhD
Research Director – Teaching and Leadership
Australian Council *for* Educational Research

References

Dinham, S 2007a, 'The dynamics of creating and sustaining learning communities', *Unicorn Online Refereed Article*, ORA43, pp. 1–16.

Dinham, S 2007b, 'How schools get moving and keep improving: Leadership for teacher learning, student success and school renewal', *Australian Journal of Education*, (in press).

Dinham, S 2005, 'Principal leadership for outstanding educational outcomes', *Journal of Educational Administration*, vol. 43, no. 4, pp. 338–56.

Hargreaves, A 1994, *Changing Teachers, Changing Times*. London: Cassell.

Voulalas, ZD, & Sharpe, F 2005, 'Creating schools as learning communities: Obstacles and processes', *Journal of Educational Administration*, vol. 43, no. 2, pp. 187–208.

Watson, K, & Steele, F 2006, 'Building a teacher education community: Recognising the ecological reality of sustainable collaboration', *Asia-Pacific Forum on Science Learning and Teaching*, vol. 7, no. 1, viewed 2007, <http://www.ied.edu.hk/apfslt/v7_issue1/watson/watson2.htm>

Contents

Foreword	*v*
Figures	*xi*
Series overview	*xii*
About the authors	*xiii*

Part I

Elizabeth Kleinhenz — 1

1	Introduction	3
2	What does research tell us about school cultures?	5
3	A professional learning culture	8
4	What does research tell us about improving the *performance* of schools and teachers?	14
5	'Managing' teachers' 'performance'	17
6	Characteristics of schools that have strong professional learning and performance cultures	23
7	Leadership	26
8	Practical ways of implementing research-based knowledge about effective learning and performance cultures: what can principals do?	31
9	Some more research-based suggestions for principals	34
10	Conclusion	36

Part II

John Fleming — 39

1	Introduction	41
2	Setting the scene: Bellfield Primary School 1992–2005	42
3	School improvement	46

4   A professional learning and performance culture   56
5   Bellfield 2005   81
6   Some thoughts on leadership   85
7   Haileybury 2006   89
8   Postscript   91

Appendix 1: Teacher excellence   *93*
Appendix 2: Induction program timetable   *95*
Appendix 3: Professional development strategy   *99*
Appendix 4: Annual professional development plan   *101*
Appendix 5: Key curriculum area recommendations (2005)   *103*
Appendix 6: Performance and development culture
questionnaire report (April 2005)   *106*
Appendix 7: Teacher performance and appraisal 2006   *108*
References   *109*

Figures

Figure 1 Sample of professional development from Bellfield
      Primary School   58

Figure 2 Information for staff about the partners' professional
      development program at Bellfield   66

Figure 3 Sample PD template of individual teacher's plan at
      Haileybury College   69

Figure 4 Sample classroom visits check list,
      Haileybury College   73

Figure 5 Outline of staff professional development process,
      Bellfield Primary School   76

Figure 6 Detail of staff professional development process,
      Bellfield Primary School   77

Figure 7 Emphasising continual improvement,
      Haileybury College   90

Series overview

The *Educational Leadership Dialogues* series is part of two core commitments by ACER Press, the publishing arm of the Australian Council *for* Educational Research: first, the series creates a bridge between educational research and practice; second, it provides resources that support educational leaders.

Our intention is to team up ACER researchers and experienced school principals to write a series of short, evidence-based, practical guides on topics of significance for schools leaders. Subjects to be covered include performance development, leadership, school improvement, mentoring and coaching, using ICT and management issues.

We were able to identify a number of highly successful principals known for their interest in particular areas and team them with well-regarded ACER researchers who had conducted research and published work in those same areas. In creating these 'teams', we realised that rather than producing texts with a single, practical voice, we also had the opportunity to create a platform for a rich dialogue between practitioner and researcher. With significant areas of agreement and disagreement or difference of focus, this conversation provides a valuable framework for both school leadership (principals, aspiring principals and other school leaders) and the research and policy community (researchers, writers, government and systems people) to explore and to debate some of the critical educational issues of our time.

Brian Caldwell, in his book *Re-imagining Educational Leadership*, explores the idea that the basic unit of organisation in the 21st century is not the school, not the class, not the subject, but the individual student. Ultimately, everything that is done in education should be about individual student outcomes. In supporting, valuing and engaging the critical issues of school leadership, this series aims to contribute to precisely that goal.

Ralph Saubern
General Manager
ACER Press

About the authors

Dr Elizabeth Kleinhenz has many years experience as a teacher, administrator, and curriculum consultant in the Victorian state education system. She is currently an ACER Senior Research Fellow.

At ACER she has provided consultancy services to various education stakeholders, including Teaching Australia, the Victorian Institute of Teaching; the Catholic Education Commission of Victoria; and the New South Wales Institute of Teachers, in the areas of teaching standards, pre-service teacher education, teacher professional development and teacher evaluation.

Previously, Kleinhenz managed the Southern Regional Information Network for LOTE, a network that brought together teachers, administrators, policy-makers and LOTE educators from many settings. She was also an assistant principal in charge of curriculum and teacher professional development at the Victorian School of Languages (VSL), where she developed comprehensive programs and processes for the professional development and performance of several hundred language teachers including the development of major projects and courses that broke new ground in the use of electronic and Computer Assisted Learning for languages.

John Fleming, from Melbourne, Victoria, taught in the Victorian government school system for nearly 30 years. He is currently Head of Precinct at the Berwick Campus of Haileybury College, on the outskirts of Melbourne. Fleming was previously principal of Bellfield Primary School, where he was committed to changing the culture of the school, and to dealing with significant literacy and numeracy challenges. He led whole-school implementation of shared teaching and learning strategies and professional development and mentoring for teachers. Fleming also introduced a structured, sequential, data-driven curriculum.

Fleming received an Award for Educational Leadership from the Australian College of Educational Leaders in 2003. He has also participated in many forums including the launch of Teaching Reading, the final report of the National Inquiry into the Teaching of Literacy, and the Ministerial

Council on Education, Employment, Training and Youth Affairs. In 2006 he was presented with the Bruce Wicking Award by Learning Difficulties Australia for services to children with special needs and with the federal Minister of Education's Special Achievement Award for his contribution to literacy and numeracy.

Part I

Elizabeth Kleinhenz

1

Introduction

The *Oxford Companion to the English Language* points out that there are two current meanings of the word 'culture'. The first, which had its origins in 'culturing' or 'tilling' the soil, continues in the sense of raising animals or plants, and in the 'culturing' of tissues for scientific purposes. The idea of growth, training and development also persists in such phrases as 'a cultured manner' or 'physical culture'. This idea is also evident in the second meaning of 'culture', which 'refers to a social condition or way of life, as seen also in the more focused terms *ancient Greek culture* and *Maori culture*' which usually have a language component (McArthur 1992). A culture in this sense refers to speaking, behaving and thinking in ways that are shared by members of a particular group or society.

In 1959, so the *Oxford Companion* tells us, the scientist and novelist CP Snow defined 20th-century western culture in *The Two Cultures and the Scientific Revolution* as two cultures—the scientific and the literary— neither knowing much about the other: 'Those in the two cultures can't talk to each other'. We now know that, as in Snow's version of western civilisation, there can be different cultures within schools. An important aim of building a professional learning and performance culture in a school is to ensure that all of the teachers are able and happy to talk to one another other about matters of common interest and concern!

The purpose of this part is to explain what is meant by 'professional learning and performance culture' in a school, why such a culture is worth building, how it can be recognised, and how it can be achieved. Research in various areas of education has offered some important insights in this field over the past half century. In light of some of this research, the chapter looks first at the various kinds of school cultures that have been observed in schools. It then examines the concepts of professional learning and 'performance' and shows how they can be established to build a culture in which teachers and school leaders accept individual and shared responsibility for their own learning and for students' progress, and have clear ideas about how improvement can be achieved.

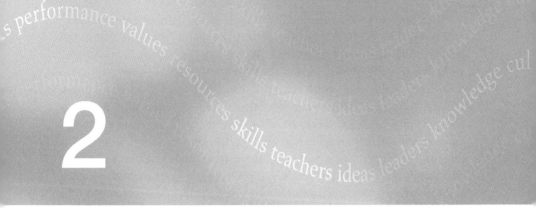

2

What does research tell us about school cultures?

'The way we do things around here'

Fullan and A Hargreaves (1991, p. 37) offer the following definition of 'culture' in schools:

> the guiding beliefs and expectations evident in the way a school operates, particularly in reference to how people relate (or fail to relate) to each other. In simple terms, culture is 'the way we do things and relate to each other around here'.

DH Hargreaves has also described school cultures as 'the knowledge, beliefs, values, customs, morals, rituals, symbols and language of a group' (1995 p. 25). Schein (1985 p. 6) sees culture as

> The deeper level of basic assumptions and beliefs that [are] shared by members of an organization, that operate unconsciously; and that define in a basic 'taken for granted' fashion an organization's view of itself and its environment.

Research tells us that some kinds of school cultures support students' learning much more strongly than others. This applies not only to whole school cultures but also to cultures within schools.

The research of Peter Hill and Ken Rowe (1995) showed that some subject departments within the same secondary schools appeared to have found more effective ways of teaching, with correspondingly better outcomes for students. Fullan and Hargreaves famously coined the term 'Balkanisation' to describe the kind of school cultures in which teachers work and socialise in exclusive groups or cliques.

Rozenholtz (1989) examined how some of the cultural characteristics of schools correlated with students' learning gains in mathematics and reading. She memorably classified the schools in her study as 'stuck', 'in-between' or 'moving'. In the 'stuck' schools, teachers rarely spoke to each other about their professional work. They worked as individuals, 'isolated' in their classrooms, and they were secretive and defensive about what went on in there. Most of these teachers were not especially interested in their own learning, and the learning of their students was sluggish. In the 'moving' schools, there were high degrees of teacher interaction that resulted in happier, more engaged teachers and students, and a greatly improved learning environment. Student achievement in the 'moving' schools was clearly higher. Measures of both teacher uncertainty and of feelings of lack of efficacy that resulted from isolation in the 'stuck' schools correlated negatively with student learning gains in reading and mathematics over a two-year period (Rozenholtz 1989 p. 128).

Interestingly, 80 per cent of the teachers in Rozenholtz's 'moving' schools saw their own professional learning as important and actively sought out opportunities for learning, especially from colleagues. These teachers worried about their performance. They thought that teaching was difficult, challenging work and that is why they felt they needed to learn how to do it better. By contrast, in the 'stuck' schools, only 17 per cent of teachers felt the need to learn from others in order to become better teachers. These teachers thought that teaching was easy!

In the nearly three decades since Rozenholtz's study, researchers have continued to find evidence of the significant contributions that 'moving' schools—schools with strong professional learning and performance cultures—make to teachers' own learning and feelings of efficacy, to the collective capacities of schools and to system-wide improvements in the practices of teaching and learning (Achinstein 2002; Grossman, Wineburg & Woolworth 2001; Gutiérrez 1996; Little 1990; Louis & Kruse 1995; McLaughlin & Talbert 2001; Newmann 1999; Stokes 2001; Talbert 1995).

Stoll (2003 pp. 59–61) expanded Rozenholtz's 'moving' and 'stuck' models into four categories.

1   **The moving school.** Moving schools have a strong sense of shared purpose. Teachers continually examine their practice and make sure that it is continuing to meet students' needs. Support is always available for collaborative efforts. People 'know where they are going and have systems and the will and the skill to get there'.

2   **The cruising school.** Cruising schools are usually located in more affluent areas. They tend to look good, usually having modern buildings and well-maintained grounds and facilities. They may be

effective in terms of student achievement, but the successful learning may be happening in spite of teacher quality. Teachers in a cruising school do not usually wish to change because of 'powerful norms of contentment'. Data based on absolute achievement rather than 'value added' give an appearance of effectiveness that appears to justify claims that the school is working well as it is. Such schools, says Stoll, may well be 'society's greatest challenge' because they have not been identified as ineffective for a significant percentage of their students.

3   **The sinking school.** Sinking schools are failing in terms of their students' achievement. Teachers do not wish to make changes, because of apathy or ignorance or both. The culture is one of isolation and blame. These schools are usually, but not always, in socially disadvantaged areas. Teachers often blame students' failure on factors outside the school.

4   **The struggling school.** Struggling schools are ineffective but improving. Staff often lack the knowledge and skills necessary for improvement but they keep trying.

> *Considerable unproductive thrashing about occurs as those in the school community determine the what and the how of the change process, and build the climate that will support other improvement conditions and strategies. There is willingness, however, to try anything that might make a difference.*

The good news for struggling schools is that they probably will get better. The bad news is that they are often seen as failing or sinking. This is very dispiriting and may impede improvement.

There is now little or no doubt that schooling is improved when teachers collectively examine new conceptions about teaching, question ineffective practices and actively support each other's professional growth.

3

A professional learning culture

What does research tell us about teachers' professional knowledge and skills?

A great deal has been said and written about professional learning and development cultures and communities in schools. The terms 'professional learning' and 'professional development' are often used interchangeably. I prefer the term 'learning' over 'development' for two reasons: first, because it seems to be more reflective of the extent and depth of what teachers need to know and do if they are to become accomplished in their craft; and because it suggests that it is the teacher—the person—who is taking charge of the activity. The notion of learning as a private as well as a community endeavour is one that should never be lost sight of.

Unfortunately, much of the talk about teachers' professional learning seriously underestimates the complexity of the teaching knowledge base. Teachers' professional development is seen as something to be 'planned' or 'managed' without proper consideration being given to *what* is to be developed, beyond 'implementing' a particular program or centrally developed initiative.

Such approaches are now recognised as short-sighted and self-defeating. A professional learning culture in a school will not even get off the ground until school leaders, in particular, develop properly sophisticated understandings of what it is that teachers need to learn. Professional knowledge and skills are at the core of any professional learning culture. After all, how can we learn if we do not know what it is that we are supposed to be learning? How can we get better if we do not know what it is that we should get better at?

The concept of a 'professional' culture entails that practitioners *share* a complex knowledge base or 'shared technical culture'. This concept is true of all professions—we do not expect, for example, that different surgeons will have different knowledge of human anatomy or that individual doctors will decide for themselves how blood circulates around the body. But—at least until recently—there has been little evidence to suggest that most teachers know and share a professional knowledge base. In 1975 Lortie, in a classic study, interviewed 94 elementary and secondary teachers in the greater Boston area ('the five towns sample'), and collected questionnaires from almost 6000 teachers in Dade County, Florida. He found teachers' work to be characterised by individualism, ambiguity and 'ad-hocness' rather than shared professional understandings and reflection. The teachers in his study reported that they rarely talked to each other about how they helped students to learn. 'Professional' conversations were confined to sharing a few practical hints and 'tricks of the trade', mostly in relation to issues of classroom and student management.

Lortie's findings were upheld by those of many subsequent studies that also failed to discover evidence of a shared knowledge base or professional culture among teachers. McAnninch (1993 p. 60) described teachers' world view as being characterised by pragmatism, individualism and a general disinclination to develop or share new knowledge. This orientation, she claimed, 'has many specific weaknesses that greatly limit the capacity of individual teachers and the occupation as a whole to advance'.

The effects of isolation and privatism on teachers' learning and professional knowledge

Historically, many new teachers have started their careers in schools where the dominant culture was one of isolation and privacy of practice. Inadequately trained to start with, they could 'teach' for their entire careers in total ignorance of new research about teaching or their disciplines (a notion that would be horrifying in any other profession), developing a private ragbag of short-term strategies to solve immediate problems without ever having an opportunity for constructive discussion with or feedback from colleagues.

Lortie (1975) coined the term 'egg crate' to describe a culture of teaching in which individual teachers took shelter in their cell-like classrooms, defending themselves against perceived invasions of their privacy. Powerful norms supported these cultures. To this day, many secondary school teachers in Australia would not dream of going into a colleague's classroom unless specifically invited.

The cultures of the 'stuck' schools in Rozenholtz's and subsequent studies in similar vein were characterised by teacher isolation and privatisation of practice. Such cultures, it has now been conclusively shown, do not help to improve the learning outcomes of students. Neither are they conducive to the development of a satisfied and productive teacher workforce.

Hargreaves and Fullan (1998 p. 6) see the problem of isolation as essential to overcome, if essential changes in teaching and learning are to occur.

> *The problem of isolation is a deep-seated one. Architecture often supports it. The timetable reinforces it. Overload sustains it. History legitimates it. Later we will review evidence that links the widespread presence of isolation and privatism to safer, less risk-taking methods of teaching and to poorer standards of student achievement. We therefore believe that cracking the walls of privatism is one of the basic issues worth fighting for. There is simply not enough opportunity and not enough encouragement for teachers to work together, learn from each other, and improve their expertise as a community.*

Advances in knowledge about teaching

A major shift in ways of thinking about teachers' knowledge, and in research on 'quality' or 'effective' teaching took place during the 1980s when the research focus moved from the classroom behaviour of teachers and its presumed effects on students' learning (the 'process–product' tradition) to a greater interest in how teachers' knowledge and thinking shapes their planning and actions in the classroom. Teachers themselves became more actively involved in this type of research than they had been in the process–product research. It turned out, for example, that teachers' knowledge and beliefs about the subject matter they were teaching had a highly significant influence on the quality of their pedagogy. Brophy (1991) contains a wide range of studies in this vein, and this research tradition continues strongly, as indicated in the latest *Handbook of Research on Teaching* (Richardson 2001).

In 1987 Lee Shulman coined the phrase 'pedagogical content knowledge' to capture the kind of knowledge teachers acquire that enables them to help students learn relevant content, whether early years' literacy or university-level economics.

This is the kind of research-based knowledge that is useful to teachers. It is properly researched knowledge that is as different from the idiosyncratic folk wisdom of the past that was the product of teachers' isolation in their classrooms, as is the application of leeches from giving penicillin to cure infection. It is this kind of research-based knowledge that teachers can share—and to which they can contribute, in highly significant ways, in professional learning cultures in their schools.

What does research tell us about effective professional learning?

McRae et al. (2001) found that 75 per cent of Australian teachers spent fewer than six days each year in professional development activities. And each activity was usually no more than two days, too short a time to lead to any significant change in practice—which research indicates is more likely with courses more than 80 hours long and extended in time (Garet et al. 2001). Significant changes in practice that lead to improved opportunities for students to learn take years of engagement in many modes of professional learning. While there are, in Australia, many individually effective professional development programs and activities operating at school and system levels, the overall pattern of provision is brief, fragmentary and rarely sequential.

In other professions there is a stronger sense of shared responsibility for professional learning. While employing authorities undoubtedly have a responsibility to provide the professional learning necessary to implement reforms that they have initiated, professional associations in other professions usually take responsibility for ensuring that individual members keep up with and develop toward professional standards. An important question to be asked of the teaching profession and of professional communities in schools is: how strong is the sense of ownership and responsibility for professional learning among teachers and their communities of practice?

Recent research on effective professional learning

A key message from research is that professional developers should create contexts and use any methods that increase the frequency and quality of professional conversations that teachers can have with each other about the content of what they are teaching, and the learning that is going on in their own classrooms. These conversations should be about deep aspects of teachers' practice—of what they could expect to get better at—that can only occur over time and as a result of reflection. Examples might include

- deeper understanding of content from the learner's point of view
- deeper knowledge and awareness of students as individuals
- capacity to provide useful feedback
- learning how to let the teacher's own authority 'go' to promote independent thinking and learning by students
- ability to make assessment a vehicle for student learning.

Effective professional learning as a long-term personal quest

Hawley and Valli (1999) speak of 'an almost unprecedented consensus' among researchers, professional development specialists and key policy-makers about how best to improve the knowledge of educators. This consensus rests on an understanding that teachers learn most effectively when they collegially engage in solving authentic problems that are related to narrowing the gaps between what students are expected to learn and their actual performance.

On the basis of several syntheses of research, Hawley and Valli identify nine 'characteristics' or 'principles' of effective professional learning that are most likely to contribute to improved teaching practice that leads to improved student learning. (These are shown in the box.)

Principles for the design of effective professional learning

1 The content of professional development focuses on what students are to learn and how to deal with the different problems students may have in learning the material.

2 Professional development should be based on analyses of the differences between actual student performance, and goals and standards for student learning.

3 Professional development should involve teachers in the identification of what they need to learn and in the development of the learning experiences in which they will be involved.

4 Professional development should be primarily school-based and built into the day-to-day work of teaching.

5 Professional development should be organised around collaborative problem-solving.

6 Professional development should be continuous and ongoing, involving follow-up and support for further learning—including support from sources external to the school that can provide necessary resources and new perspectives.

7 Professional development should incorporate evaluation of multiple sources of information on outcomes for students, and the instruction and other processes that are involved in implementing the lessons learned through professional development.

8 Professional development should provide opportunities to gain an understanding of the theory underlying the knowledge and skills being learned.

9 Professional development should be connected to a comprehensive change process focused on improving student learning.

(Hawley & Valli 1999)

Hawley and Valli's first principle emphasises the overriding importance of *what* teachers learn, as well as *how* they learn it. As Kennedy (1999) puts it, the *form* of professional learning is less important than the *what*—the substance or content. It turns out that knowledge is the key when it comes to professional learning, particularly when it leads to deeper understanding of the content that students are to learn, the research on how students learn that content, and the nature of the problems different students have in learning that content.

Hawley and Valli's second principle emphasises the importance of focusing professional learning around data and feedback from one's own students, especially data about where those students are in relation to where they could or should be in their development. Some of the most effective professional learning now comes through activities that help teachers to 'moderate' or compare their own students' work with that of students taught by other teachers.

The third principle asks teachers to identify 'gaps' in their own learning. This is a valuable learning experience in itself, as is choosing the learning experiences that they will need to deal with these gaps. Teachers are used to doing this for their students, so they should have little difficulty in going through similar processes for their own learning.

The fourth and fifth principles build on long experience that has told us the most effective professional learning happens in schools as teachers work together on authentic teaching tasks and problems.

The sixth and seventh principles show the importance of allowing sufficient time and support, including support from outside the school, and of allowing time to evaluate the professional development itself. Evaluation of professional development yields important lessons for refining further professional development activities. Without such evaluation, future opportunities for teachers to learn may not be productive.

The eighth principle relates closely to the first. Changes in practice are more likely to be sustained when they are informed by theory in which the teacher has confidence. This principle is also connected to the ninth, which shows that teachers' capabilities will not improve unless the conditions that influence improvement are dealt with. These conditions include time and opportunities to try new practices, funding and technical assistance. If professional development is not designed to be part of a larger change process, it is unlikely to be effective.

The importance of making teachers' practice the site for professional learning is inherent in all nine of the Hawley and Valli principles. Practice-based professional learning represents a major shift from traditional views of professional learning that is based on participation in 'courses'. This is not to imply that courses and other activities such as workshops and conferences do not have an important role in supporting professional learning but these activities are only the 'front end' of improving the work of teachers. We have known for a long time that the 'back end' of processes of change and improvement is where the hard work has to be done—supporting teachers as they test new approaches in their own classrooms (Fullan 1982). Effective systems of professional learning are practice-based. As such, they reflect the best principles of what is currently known about effective professional learning.

4

What does research tell us about improving the *performance* of schools and teachers?

The notion of improving school performance and developing a 'performance culture' has borrowed from the business community the notion of 'outputs'. At its core is the not unreasonable expectation that schools should be able to 'perform'—that is, that teachers and school leaders should provide an account of what, and how well, students are learning in comparison with 'benchmarks' that provide an indication of what they 'should' be learning. The focus, in a school that is concerned about performance, is no longer solely on examining 'inputs'—for example, syllabuses, teaching methods and philosophies (although these things, of course, remain important)—it is on how the learning of students has improved as a result of those inputs. As we might question whether a salesperson, no matter how skilled, who never makes a sale can justifiably still claim to be a salesperson or whether a business that fails to produce goods that people want to buy is viable, so the idea of 'outputs' raises questions about schools and teachers whose students fail to learn.

This question is taken up in a recent article (Masters 2005) which pointed to the occurrence, during the 20th century, of a major shift in thinking about education that had important effects on ideas about schools' performance and accountability. In essence, the shift was a change in focus from what and how was being *taught* to whether and how students were *learning*. This change, said Masters, has meant the end of the days where teachers could take comfort in only having taught—or 'covered'—a syllabus or course of study. In the 21st century, he says, schools and teachers will know and take individual and collective responsibility for the extent to which students have *learnt* what has been taught. This is the main feature that will distinguish schools that have a culture of 'performance' from those that do not. Actual, measurable student achievement is now a phenomenon that bears a direct relation to what schools and teachers do.

> *During the twentieth century, educators Ralph Tyler, Benjamin Bloom and others underscored the observation that schooling is fundamentally about children learning. More important than the question of whether and what teachers have taught is the question of whether and what students have learnt. Of course, these are related: if teachers are not teaching, then students are unlikely to be learning. But it was an important shift to put student learning at the heart of the education process. From the point of view of accountability, it was no longer sufficient to know that teachers had taught the syllabus (input); the more important question was what progress students had made (output).*

(Masters 2005 p. 1)

Teachers will be quick to perceive, and Masters and other writers on this subject will readily acknowledge, that extreme caution is required in this field. Experience has shown, and research has demonstrated, that measuring teacher and school effectiveness according to student achievement is not nearly as easy as it appears. Many things affect what students learn, apart from teachers, and it is always the case that students' learning results from of the work of not one teacher but many. Sometimes the influence of one teacher may not be apparent for a number of years: most of us know stories about people who in adult life took up study or a project because of interest that was kindled many years ago by one of their teachers. Students learn from television, films, books, the Internet and their peers. The influence of home, family and the students' own interests and abilities have all been shown to be significant factors in learning.

The fact remains, however, that improving student learning and achievement is the core business of schools. This calls for quality teaching; 'performing' schools are quick to recognise this. Teachers and school leaders accept responsibility and are prepared to be accountable for the extent and nature of the improvements they effect in learning and teaching.

In order to improve student achievement, teachers need to know at what level their students are for particular stages of their learning and they need to know how to help students to move on and improve. They then need to know how to assess or measure that improvement and to reflect on the elements of their teaching that have caused the improvement to occur. As they do these things, they develop their own professional learning (as discussed earlier). Knowing at what level students are working, monitoring their improvement, and focusing on the gaps between current achievements and goals and the activities that help them to improve are thus key elements of a professional learning and performance culture in a school.

While it is certainly true that many things influence students' learning, teachers and schools need to know and to be accountable for what *they* contribute—what has been called 'added value'—to students' learning. Schools that can justly claim to have improved the learning of a majority of their students, independently of background and other variables can claim to be 'strongly performing' schools. In such schools teachers *collectively and individually* accept responsibility for what and how their students have learnt and are able to give an account—to be accountable—for that learning and how they have helped to bring it about.

Such schools can legitimately lay claim to possessing a 'professional learning and performance culture'.

5

'Managing' teachers' 'performance'

In recent years, new understandings about teachers' own learning and about effective organisational management have caused education systems to investigate various ways of combining professional learning with accountability in order to improve the performance of individuals and schools. Chief of these is performance management and appraisal, the main objectives of which are to improve teachers' professional learning and to provide public guarantees that teachers are working effectively in accordance with both school goals and those of the education system.

The management literature shows that considerable progress has been made in managing the performance of individuals within various organisations and systems. When investigating the performance management system currently in operation in Victorian government schools, the Boston Consulting Group (2003 p. 24) found that many of the 'right' components were in place:

> the elements of the system in large part match those we see in a range of organisations with effective performance management systems, and which academics and other experts cite as the 'ideal' performance management system for teachers and schools.

But then, the Boston Group found that

> In practice . . . the performance management system does not work in most schools . . . Schools see the process as cumbersome and low value, and many teachers do not see it as constructive. Very strong teachers tend to characterise the process as a waste of time, while less strong teachers may question the school leader's ability to provide them with effective feedback.

This finding agreed with research conducted in 2002, in which teachers and principals in primary and secondary Victorian schools reported their experiences of performance management (Kleinhenz & Ingvarson 2004). The schools were investing considerable energy and resources into their performance management systems but the results, when measured against the goals of the systems, were disappointing. Most teachers and school administrators did not believe that processes were making any significant contributions to teachers' professional learning, or that the processes provided more than basic guarantees of competency. The main emphasis appeared to be on setting up reasonably efficient systems and on making the contact between reviewee and reviewer as easy, 'comfortable' and 'unthreatening' as possible, within the limits of meeting the education system's expectations for compliance.

There was one strange finding. In the secondary schools, the people who 'reviewed' the performance of their colleagues more often than not did not teach in the same subject area or at the same year levels. Reviewers and reviewees often had little to do with each other, professionally or socially, in the normal course of the school week, term and year. They just met a couple of times to fulfil the requirements of the performance management process, ticking the relevant boxes as necessary. The reviewer was usually a person who was senior in the school's hierarchy but not necessarily one who had involvement in the reviewee's work. In fact, more than one teacher said that they had 'chosen' their reviewer on the grounds that he or she knew little about their area of teaching because they felt 'more comfortable' with such a person. This may well have been so but it considerably limited the capacity of the review process to fulfil its two major goals: helping teachers to learn and providing an accurate account of their contributions to the improvement of students' learning.

These schools were not, to use Rozenholtz's terminology, 'stuck'. The local regional authorities had recommended them for study as schools that offered models of effective practice. Other evidence suggested that they were well on the way to becoming strong professional learning communities. Teachers were already learning and working together in teams, and it seemed that it would not have been difficult to integrate performance management into the existing professional learning structures by, for example, allowing team leaders to mentor and to monitor the learning and professional growth of team members.

There may well have been good reasons for the principals and teachers not choosing to go down this path. It is not part of the purpose of this section to interrogate these reasons. It needs only to be noted that effective performance management is, or can become, an important component of a professional learning and performance culture, one that can strengthen the whole in highly significant ways. Research tells us that teachers are fully prepared to be accountable; it is not the fact of accountability itself but the ways in which it is often demanded that cause the problems.

Teachers are particularly dismissive of 'tick the box' approaches that fail to acknowledge the depth and complexity of their work (McLaughlin & Pfeiffer 1988 p. 2).

Developers of performance management schemes are now beginning to recognise that schools cannot 'implement' them if they do not have the capacity to do so. This means much more than 'setting effective systems in place', although that is usually a good idea too. Building schools' capacity to effectively 'manage' performance means, at the very least, that everyone needs to have a clear understanding of what they are doing and why. Developing sophisticated understandings of what teachers know and do, and building performance management arrangements around these understandings is a highly complex and challenging endeavour that needs to take place in the kind of context that is generally provided by a strong professional learning and performance culture.

Building a school's capacity to carry out performance management effectively entails building on and developing various components of the culture, such as team learning. It requires, especially, respect for teachers' learning and this, as has been shown, means that teachers and school leaders need to respect and understand the professional knowledge base— not trivialise or ignore it. Trivialisation is exactly what happens when, for example, a senior science teacher is called upon to review the performance of a teacher of music or French, in isolation and with minimal reference to the relevant professional knowledge. Examples like this, of which there appear to be far too many in school performance review systems, reflect a serious misunderstanding and undervaluing of teachers' work.

'Compliance' and 'commitment'

The notion of 'compliance' is closely linked with the ways in which work is understood—or misunderstood. Insistence on compliance, as opposed to encouragement of commitment, is related to a failure to properly understand what teachers know and do. It may well be at the core of long-standing problems with 'managing' the performance of teachers, in the sense that teachers' work has rarely been understood as truly professional work. Darling-Hammond (1988) pointed out that compliance is a feature of 'bureaucratic' rather than 'professional' accountability. Bureaucratic systems, she says (1988 p. 11), are suitable for work in which goals are uncomplicated and the procedures for reaching goals are consistent and uniform. In bureaucratic systems, workers need only be monitored for compliance with preset rules and guidelines. If something goes wrong under this system, if the end product does not meet expectations, it can only be said that the specifications are faulty or incomplete or that the worker has failed to comply.

Holding teachers responsible only for compliance, says Darling-Hammond (1988 p. 11), is obviously unsatisfactory because it removes from them all responsibility for developing their knowledge about teaching. It also removes their responsibility for being genuinely and directly accountable for the learning and welfare of the children they teach: 'The standard for compliance becomes compliance rather than effectiveness'. A compliance model of teacher performance management defeats its own main purposes. Teachers do not learn from it. Neither does it provide them with opportunities to demonstrate how they take responsibility for improving the learning of their students. It encourages the exact opposite of a model of a professional learning and performance culture in which teachers assume individual and collective responsibility for their own learning and for improvement in their students' learning. Compliance is the opposite of commitment.

Under a professional model, Darling-Hammond continues, teachers would be more directly accountable to their students and their families. They would also be accountable to their colleagues and professional communities for upholding professionally agreed standards of practice. This model involves building teachers' *personal commitment* to helping students succeed rather than demanding compliance with external, hierarchical requirements. A powerful justification for this commitment model, she claims, is that it leads, as a bureaucratic-compliance model cannot, to expanded knowledge about teaching, better-prepared teachers and a more appropriate student–teacher relationship.

Professional teaching standards

With the establishment of institutes and colleges of teaching in all Australian states and territories (except the ACT, although it is moving strongly in this direction), the 'standards movement' has gained momentum in recent years, as each of these bodies has developed sets of professional teaching standards that are used to register teachers. Some of these state bodies have also developed, or are planning to develop, standards for accrediting teacher education courses.

In 2003 the Ministerial Council on Education, Employment, Training and Youth Affairs published *A National Framework for Professional Standards for Teaching*. This was the culmination of work sponsored, in particular, by the Australian Council of Educators. It claims to provide 'an organisational structure which establishes, at a national level, the agreed foundational elements and dimensions of effective teaching'.

Various sets of 'professional' teaching standards have also been developed, nationally and internationally, by employers of teachers for various purposes including performance management. These standards tend to vary in quality. Few, if any, succeed in fully articulating the elements of a professional knowledge base of teaching.

Standards developed by employers for purposes of performance management in Australian and overseas education systems have a poor record in terms of being accepted by teachers and helping them to learn. They are all too often presented in the form of generic 'check lists' of relatively simple teacher 'behaviours' that lend themselves to quick and easy 'measurement' of teachers' performance by managers who may not have expertise in the field of teaching they are assessing. It does need to be said that even such rudimentary sets of standards are probably better than no standards at all. Most of them do, at least, give teachers some idea of the areas in which they may need to improve.

The rationale for well-developed professional teaching standards is that they provide teachers with a 'map' of what it is that they should get better at, thereby establishing a powerful framework for teachers' professional learning. When the conditions are right, standards help teachers to give each other feedback on their performances. They also enable and empower teachers to provide accurate accounts of their own development in evaluation processes that guarantee the effectiveness of their practice.

> *Standards clarify what teachers should get better at over the long term. Standards describe trajectories for professional development. They make manifest the idea that good teaching is something a person learns how to do over time; that good teaching is not just a bundle of personality traits. Standards confront the mindset that teaching is just a matter of personal styles and doing your own thing.*
>
> *Standards give warrant to the claim that teaching is a profession with the capacity to evaluate its own practice and implement professional models of accountability. Standards provide a foundation for teachers and their associations to provide leadership in their own profession.*

(Ingvarson 2001 pp. 4–5)

Simplistic check lists of generic 'standards' statements, written in dot-point form, will not serve these purposes, although they may be useful for evaluating basic competence. Like the inadequate performance management processes they so often underpin, such lists tend to trivialise and to undervalue teachers' work. But it is no easy task to develop standards that do succeed in providing full and accurate representations of the knowledge and wisdom of teachers. For this reason, the 'best' sets of standards are those developed by teachers themselves, and for which teachers assume 'ownership' and responsibility.

In the United States, standards development groups with a majority of teacher members have now developed professional teaching standards for accomplished teaching in nearly 30 fields, under the auspices of the National Board for Professional Teaching Standards (NBPTS). Teachers may voluntarily apply to become 'certified' according to these standards in evaluation processes, external to schools, in which they are assessed not by managers but by their peers. Science teachers assess science teachers, music teachers assess music teachers and so on. Teachers who have been able to demonstrate, in these rigorous peer assessment processes, that they meet the standards are in very high demand in schools across the United States, because the standards and evaluation processes are recognised to be authentic and demanding.

The work of the NBPTS reflects an understanding that teaching is complex professional work and that profession-developed and profession-owned standards can form the basis of professional accountability models in which teachers are committed to and take responsibility for their own learning and performance. This understanding also lies at the heart of professional learning and performance cultures in schools.

Three field-specific sets of standards, similar to NBPTS standards, have now been developed in Australia by the Australian Science Teachers Association (ASTA), the Australian Association for the Teaching of English (AATE) and the Australian Literacy Educators' Association (ALEA), and the Australian Association of Mathematics Teachers (AAMT). They are readily accessible on the associations' websites. This extract from the standards for teachers of science demonstrates, as most examples of employer-developed standards do not, a deep and broad understanding of what it is that highly accomplished science teachers know and can do:

> *Highly accomplished teachers of science engage their students in drawing evidence-based conclusions and being able to justify these conclusions taking into account societal and cultural values and environmental considerations as well as scientific information. Their students often engage in problem solving activities—recognising and defining problems and putting forward plans to address them. Students in their classes, no matter what age, weigh up evidence and ask 'what's fair?' and 'what's reasonable?'*

> (Australian Science Teachers Association 2002)

Schools that are developing their professional learning and performance cultures need to be aware of these sets of profession-developed and profession-owned standards and their potential to aid teachers' learning. Teachers and school leaders should also ensure that they keep abreast of the fast-moving national 'standards agenda' in Australia. One good way of doing this is through the professional associations.

Characteristics of schools that have strong professional learning and performance cultures

What would a school with a strong professional learning and performance culture look like? If a teacher, researcher, or other educational professional were to spend, say three weeks in a school with such a culture, what might he or she expect to see and experience? The following model for such a culture was developed on the basis of the research and writing discussed in earlier sections. The model also draws heavily on the work of Peter Senge (1990) and Isaacson and Bamburg (1992).

People enjoy learning

Teachers and school leaders are intelligent people who like to grow personally as well as professionally. They are collegiate, but they also see learning as an individual, private experience. The leadership encourages teachers to question, to seek truth, to assume responsibility and to pursue the things that are most important to them. The success of the individual is regarded as important as the success of the whole school, and learning is recognised as being at least as important to the individual as it is to the organisation.

People treat each other with respect

Teachers and school leaders agree about the goals and purposes of teaching, and of the school, although there is always room for healthy debate. Most importantly they share a belief that everyone should take individual and collective responsibility for successful learning by students. This responsibility is strongly tied to a sense of personal responsibility and to a shared understanding that individual teachers, their colleagues and the school as a whole are accountable for the quality of students' learning. This understanding is related to the belief that every child can learn.

The knowledge and skills of experienced teachers are valued and strong support is provided for new teachers

A strong learning and performance culture is forward looking but this does not mean that it dismisses or undervalues the knowledge and skills of its most experienced members. Experienced teachers contribute strongly to joint work and shared growth and development in their work areas and the school as a whole. They play a major role, especially, in the induction and mentoring of new teachers, who are offered every support in their early years of teaching.

Teachers and school leaders have common, well-articulated understandings about how the future of the school will be shaped

The unfortunate thing about the 'fashionable issue' of shared vision, say Isaacson and Bamburg (1992), is that it has come to mean that a set of beliefs and ideas developed by some person who is senior in an organisation's hierarchy, such as a principal, is somehow communicated to others in the organisation who are then expected to share and implement it. Such 'visions' tend to defeat their own purposes. Isaacson and Bamburg support Senge's contention that a vision should never be imposed:

> The result of those (imposed) activities is rampant cynicism; educators believe that their organizations either will never really serve causes they believe in, that they will have to be effective in spite of the institution, or that what they care most about will ultimately be damaged or destroyed. 'This too shall pass' becomes the belief of frustrated idealists.

(Senge 1990 p. 44)

Instead, shared vision that truly encompasses the personal visions of all members of the organisation can 'become the heart of a learning organisation'.

Teachers and school leaders constantly question mental models and assumptions that may impede progress and change

Isaacson and Bamburg (1992) suggest that seeing students' minds as 'empty vessels to be filled with knowledge' is an example of a 'mental model' that has 'profoundly affected what has happened in classrooms since the founding of our current educational system'. Questioning this mental model, they say, 'offers the opportunity to share our assumptions about children, learning instructional strategies, curriculums, relationships with parents, and the school calendar and schedule—even furniture and architecture'. Questioning this and other mental models, these writers claim, allows teachers to 'share a new language; talk together in new ways about our values, assumptions and beliefs; and collaboratively create new inventions we hadn't previously considered' (p. 43).

Teachers and school leaders constantly engage in joint work or 'teaming'

Recognising the large body of research that shows how learning and decision making are most effectively carried out in small work-teams, Isaacson and Bamburg support Senge's belief that it is time that learning was redefined to include the collective learning of groups. Attending only to the learning of individuals, they say, is 'analogous to teaching discrete basketball manoeuvres to players and then expecting them to know how to win games when they're all out on the court together' (1992 p. 44). The discipline of team learning, they say, builds upon the discipline of personal mastery. It helps teachers to think 'insightfully' about their mental models, to balance the need to be responsive to the needs and learning of others with the need to express their own points of view, and to become more effective in reaching collective goals. Team learning requires time, support and practice.

Teaming helps teachers to challenge their mental models and to examine their practices and assumptions about teaching (Schon 1987). Kruse (1997 p. 57) discovered that teachers who regularly work, learn and collaborate with other teachers are more prepared to look for new ideas and opinions about 'expert' practice. Teachers who participated in this study also reported more ownership in the classrooms and increased feeling of ownership of the school's mission.

Teachers in schools with strong professional learning and development cultures team teach, plan together, observe each other's classes and offer feedback. Importantly, they discuss examples of students' work, comparing the work of their own students with that of students taught by other teachers. They make extensive and intelligent use of data (especially student achievement data) and of feedback from their own students to move their discussions forward and to make sound, evidence-based decisions about future actions. Their analyses home in on the differences between actual student learning and goals, and the goals and standards they expect students to achieve.

7

Leadership

Excellent leadership is, perhaps the most crucial feature of a school with a strong learning and performance culture. There is a vast literature on 'leadership' (one researcher, for example, synthesised over 7000 studies). This section will cover only what seem to be the most relevant aspects of the 'territory' of leadership theory and its relationship to professional learning and performance cultures in schools.

Changing expectations of school leaders

Expectations of school principals and leaders have changed substantially over the past 30 years. This is largely the result of school self-management and the devolution of responsibilities that were formerly held by education bureaucracies.

Some of the changes stem from advances in professional knowledge based on research; others are a response to specific changes, regulations or procedures introduced by employers. School leaders are certainly much more likely to be expected to establish a professional learning and performance culture in their schools than they would have been 30 years ago. Principals and school leaders now have to manage and monitor curriculum development and assessment of student achievement within state frameworks, select teaching and other staff, and manage the performance and professional development of staff. Financial management, marketing and the building of partnerships within the school community also fall within their responsibilities.

Research conducted so far does not show that principals and deputy principals are unhappy with this situation. The Victorian Department of Education and Training's report *The Privilege and the Price* (2004), which focused mainly on principals' workload, health and wellbeing, found that principals expressed high levels of satisfaction with their jobs, although they were also concerned about the effects of stress on their health and personal and family relationships. Overwhelmingly, they also reported that they did not spend enough time on leadership of teaching and learning. Similarly, a study conducted in Queensland (Cranston et al. 2004) found that 90 per cent of government school deputy principals were satisfied or very satisfied with their role. But only half of these people said that they intended to seek promotion to principal, citing mainly the desire for sustainable work–life balance.

Changing conceptions of school leadership

Before the early 1990s the terms 'school leadership' or 'educational leadership' were rarely heard. The 'old' discourse, which is now discredited, was about 'educational administration' or 'educational management' (Grace 1995 pp. 1–2). The switch in terminology from management to leadership was important because it accompanied the important shift (discussed above) that replaced an 'input' focus on teaching and school programs with an 'output' emphasis on what students had learnt. After this shift, school principals and leaders became responsible for outcomes in terms of what the school and students had achieved and how improvement had occurred. The emphasis was on change-oriented knowledge and evidence-based performance (Murphy & Shipman 2003).

'Transformational leadership', 'distributed leadership' and 'teacher leadership'

There are now three main areas of interest in the leadership literature: 'transformational leadership', 'distributed leadership', and 'teacher leadership'. A growing number of scholars in the leadership field, especially in educational leadership, have become dissatisfied with the idea of the 'transformational' or 'charismatic' leader, who seems able to miraculously transform school cultures (Copland 2001), although this discourse still has powerful proponents. A major problem with the 'charismatic' leadership ideal is that this kind of leadership is comparatively rare while the need for strong school leaders is urgent. We need to allow for the probability that not all leaders are born. It is quite possible for lesser mortals to learn to be good leaders and it may even be that an empathetic and diligent tortoise can outperform the hare!

The idea of distributed leadership in a school may be part of a reaction against the idea of the 'heroic' or transformative principal who can 'turn schools around' all by himself or herself. Distributed leadership simply means that formal leadership roles are shared among teachers in a school, with some teachers leading others in areas where they have particular expertise, for example, literacy, numeracy, integrated curriculum or a subject specialism like history or chemistry. At the heart of the idea of distributed leadership is rejection of the leader–follower relationship in favour of one that favours collegiality and collaboration. Distributed leadership is not a hierarchical notion: the leader of integrated curriculum may also be a literacy teacher who depends on the literacy leader for advice and leadership in that area. In this sense, there will be multiple leaders in a school (Gronn 2004) and a major part of the role of the principal and deputy principal(s) will be to coordinate the leaders' work.

Proponents of 'teacher leadership' see it as closely related to, and even overlapping, that of 'distributed leadership'. The concept is also closely linked to the literature on school improvement (Day & Harris 2002 p. 958), especially the literature on how to sustain improvement (Mulford 2003 p. 2). Under this concept all teachers are leaders in that they all have a shared sense of purpose, participate in decision making, collaborate and engage in teamwork and, most importantly, accept individual and joint responsibility for the outcomes of students' learning. Again the role of the principal in a school with teacher leadership is one of coordination.

Guiding conceptions of leadership

Exercising leadership in a school setting mainly entails *mobilising* and *energising others*, with the aim of improving a school's performance in the critical areas of teaching and learning. Since improvement of a school's performance frequently involves doing things differently from how they have been done in the past, such leadership often requires managing a process of change. A hallmark of leadership is taking the initiative, an attitude of 'making it happen'.

> The litmus test of all leadership is whether it mobilises people's commitment to putting their energy into actions designed to improve things. It is individual commitment, but above all it is collective mobilisation.

> (Fullan 2001 p. 9)

Michael Fullan (2001 p. 4) has identified five 'components' of leadership:

- moral purpose
- understanding and managing change
- building and maintaining relationships
- creating and sharing knowledge
- ensuring coherence and alignment of structures.

Moral purpose

'You don't have to be Mother Teresa to have moral purpose', says Fullan (2001 p. 13). Moral purpose is critical to the success, long and short term, of all organisations. In education, it simply means that principals and teachers are committed to improving the lives and learning of the children for whom they are responsible. Leading with moral purpose has instrumental value but it is also a core value of 'authentic' leaders, who are recognisable by virtue of their integrity, reliability, sense of purpose, firmness of conviction and substance.

Understanding and managing change

Without an understanding of change, says Fullan (2001 p. 5) 'moral purpose will lead to martyrdom'. Not all change represents improvement and not every improvement requires change. Frequently, improvement occurs when leaders motivate individuals to become more skilled and thoughtful regarding their work.

Effective leaders recognise the complexities of change processes as they develop plans and marshal resources. This entails organising, usually with others, an approach to be followed, identifying needed resources, and assembling what is required.

Fullan (2001 p. 5) offers six guidelines for understanding and managing change:

- the goal is not to innovate the most
- it is not enough to have the best ideas
- appreciate early difficulties of trying something new—the 'implementation dip'
- refine resistance as a potential positive force
- reculturing is the name of the game
- never a use a check-list approach, recognise that change is always complex.

Building and maintaining relationships

'If relationships improve, things get better. If they remain the same, or get worse, ground is lost' (Fullan 2001 p. 5). Good leaders are persuasive and well able to convince others to join in the effort. They develop the interpersonal and facilitative skills of listening, joint problem-solving, honouring other people's ideas and maintaining focus but they also know when to be decisive, to cut to the heart of something and to move the group forward to action.

Creating and sharing knowledge

Leadership entails creating new knowledge, learning from experiences, synthesising and analysing the findings of research and investigation, formulating and testing hypotheses, and drawing conclusions. It also involves encouraging colleagues to take up leadership roles, and being aware of, sharing with others, and acting upon, relevant findings from research.

Ensuring coherence and alignment of structures

'All this complexity', says Fullan (2001 p. 6), 'keeps people on the edge of chaos. It is important to be on that edge, because that is where creativity resides. But anarchy lurks there too'. This is why it is so important to ensure coherence. 'Effective leaders tolerate enough ambiguity to keep the creative juices flowing, but along the way (once they and the group know enough), they seek coherence' (Fullan 2001 p. 6). New initiatives layered on one another without coherence or connection with the culture and mission of the school will collapse. Creating coherence involves establishing structures that can be sustained over time, not swept away by the next popular reform.

These five components can infuse the leadership actions of all principals and school leaders.

8

Practical ways of implementing research-based knowledge about effective learning and performance cultures: what can principals do?

Judith Warren-Little (Darling-Hammond & Sykes 1999 p. 233) claims that school organisation is commonly 'at odds' with what research tells us about effective teacher learning and development. We know that, in such cultures, teachers—at the very least—should have the time and space to talk to each other and visit each other's classrooms. But how can this be achieved?

Create opportunities for collaborative enquiry into student learning

The first thing, says Warren-Little, is to convince teachers and school leaders of the importance of the research-based proposition that professional learning occurs most powerfully when teachers systematically study students' work together and 'figure out' the various ways in which their knowledge and actions helped that learning to occur.

This makes sense. Becoming motivated makes things happen. We do not give up smoking until we are absolutely convinced that it is injurious to our health. Teachers will not want to study students' work collaboratively and systematically until they recognise how useful and important this activity is. Principals must not only make the organisational arrangements that will create time and space for this work, they must also be convinced, and be able to convince teachers, of its value.

Warren-Little suggests two ways in which this might happen. The first is to instigate research projects—she suggests a writing workshop but ICT projects are also useful examples—that make it necessary for teachers to work collaboratively. Research projects may also include partnerships with teachers in different schools, universities or other agencies. The second way is to support 'the organisational habit of shared student assessment, employing a range of evidence'. The key word here is 'habit'. Collaborative cultures grow and develop when teachers are in the habit of jointly assessing students' work.

Find structural alternatives

Quoting research that shows students' academic achievement to be higher in schools where teachers report high levels of collective responsibility for student learning, Warren-Little's next suggestion is for principals and school leaders to foster the development of *structures* that create interdependence among teachers and shared responsibility for the same groups of students. These include suggestions for what Australians would call 'mini-schools' or schools within a school: houses and teams that use shared resources and have a common focus for teaching. While she cautions that structure alone will not bring about more positive school cultures, she quotes an 'expanding case literature' that shows how shared responsibility for students grows when structure and culture reinforce one another.

Assign teachers to appropriate classes and student groups

As Warren-Little notes, research shows that teachers are often assigned to teach classes that do not match their experience and knowledge (Finley 1984; Gehrke & Sheffield 1985; Neufeld 1984; Talbert 1990) and that teacher efficacy is strongly related to the classes they teach and to how well teachers are suited to those classes (Raudenbush, Rowan & Cheong 1992). The result of mismatch is unhappy teachers and dissatisfied teacher communities.

Principals and school leaders need to be aware of and to guard against internal school political practices—such as reserving the 'best' classes for the more senior teachers in the hierarchy—that result in poor matches between teachers and their classes. They should also understand how assigning teachers to particular classes affects the relationships between teachers and the sense of professional community generally:

> teaching assignments configure teachers' relationships with colleagues in particular ways. They may preserve well-protected fiefdoms or the prerogatives of seniority—or they may configure a staff in ways that provide a basis for professional exchange, mutual support and shared enquiry. They may plunge beginning teachers into an ordeal of survival, or provide them with well-supported entry into teaching.

(Darling-Hammond & Sykes 1999 p. 241)

Provide access to information, materials and technology

The major investment in children's learning, says Warren-Little, is the teacher. Principals and school leaders should do everything in their power to ensure that teachers have access to professional and other intellectual materials inside and outside the school. These include books, journals, reference materials, access to a telephone and to the Internet. They also include curriculum materials and examples of students' and other teachers' work. Computer hardware and software should be available to support rapid advances in computer-assisted learning and teachers' own work and professional learning. When making decisions about the allocation of resources, says Warren-Little, principals should make the professional needs of teachers a priority.

Organise and use teachers' time effectively

Warren-Little challenges the 'expectation' that time for professional development and collaboration is something that is apart from or in addition to the regular work schedules of teachers. This time should be thought of as part of teachers' 'normal' work, in the same way as timetabled 'instruction' time. School timetables should make provision for it:

> Without discounting all the ways in which teachers learn on their own, both in and out of school, the central argument here is that the school's contribution to teacher learning comes largely in the form of regularly scheduled common time among teachers who share responsibility for students or who otherwise have reason to work with one another.

(Darling-Hammond & Sykes 1999 p. 243)

Studies that 'assault the schedules that bind' (Canady & Rettig 1995; Cushman 1989) and document alternative ways of timetabling and scheduling that provide teachers with more out-of-class time for collaboration (Raywid 1995) show that schools *can* change time configurations and that, when they do, there are usually benefits for students and the professional community. But case studies of three schools carried out by Peterson, McCarthey and Elmore (1996) warn that creating more collaboration time without attending to what the teachers will do in that time is likely to be unproductive. Changing schedules alone does not change the culture.

9

Some more research-based suggestions for principals

In 2002–04, Eleanor Drago-Severson (2004) conducted and reported research that examined how 25 leaders from public, Catholic, and independent schools across the United States with varying levels of financial resources understood the effectiveness of their leadership practices in supporting teachers' professional growth. This research suggests some useful strategies for principals and school leaders who aim to establish strong learning and performance cultures in their schools.

Four Pillars

The 25 principals in Drago-Severson's study used 'Four Pillars' that supported what they understood to be a new learning model:

1 teaming or partnering with colleagues within and outside the school
2 providing teachers with leadership roles
3 engaging in collegial enquiry
4 mentoring.

Drago-Severson (2004 p. 173) found that among the actions and principles considered and used by successful school leaders when building a new learning model based on these four pillars) were

- articulating thinking through writing, acting or speaking
- identifying and questioning assumptions in a supportive context
- assuming more work-related responsibility
- supporting and challenging enhanced risk-taking
- becoming more aware of one's own or another person's motivations, actions, thinking or justifications

- identifying and increasing awareness of convictions (ethical, practical, personal convictions or questions)
- creating opportunities to act on new thinking, new ideas
- increasing the potential for greater self-authorship and self-ownership.

While all principals in the study had built upon the 'Four Pillars' using, to varying extents, these principles and actions, the ways in which they did so varied according to the circumstances and particular philosophies of their individual schools.

Drago-Severson stresses that 'In the growth and development of any school, it is the growth and development of people that make the difference'. She also emphasises the need for principals and schools leaders to develop an understanding of how adults learn:

> Merely acquiring information or learning new instructional skills, while important, can never satisfy teacher growth. Support for adult learning and growth must include efforts to improve their capacities for managing the complexities of work and life.

(Drago-Severson 2004 p. 175)

School climate

All principals in Drago-Severson's study had developed their own formal and informal ways of improving school 'climate'. These were mostly obvious things like 'being visible', modelling school values (such as respect for others and lifelong learning), providing food at meetings, celebrating achievements and organising regular social gatherings. One principal concentrated on knowing and encouraging the individual intellectual and artistic qualities of her teachers:

> We also have a lot of people here who have their own work. We have artists who are working artists. We have two people in the English department who are playwrights, whose plays have been produced on and off Broadway. We have musicians who really work on their own music. We have math teachers who write textbooks . . . I think for an institution, somehow to figure out a way to support people in their own work . . . is [important].

The principals had also worked out some 'creative' strategies for finding money for teacher professional development. They included reordering priorities, locating funds from a variety of outside sources, including school alumni, and building partnerships. One principal had developed a useful reciprocal arrangement with a university in which university teachers worked with teachers in his school and he talked about 'real life in schools' with education students at the university.

10

Conclusion

Schools with strong learning and performance cultures are 'moving' schools. They are characterised by respectful and collaborative relationships among intelligent individuals who enjoy learning. Teachers and school leaders in these schools follow a professional model of accountability: they take personal and collective responsibility for improving students' learning and their own teaching practice. Improving students' learning, while giving full consideration to the full range of contextual and other influences on their lives, is understood by all to be the core purpose of education and of the school.

Teachers in schools with strong learning and performance cultures have high levels of pedagogical and content knowledge and skills that they continue to develop, individually and collaboratively, throughout their professional lives. They work and learn in teams, giving each other feedback, observing each other's teaching, and accepting feedback from colleagues, parents and their students. Principals and school leaders are accomplished teachers who understand and respect the complexity of the professional knowledge base and value teachers' work accordingly.

Principals and school leaders in schools with strong learning and performance cultures understand that the teacher is the most important influence on students' learning. They create opportunities for developing ideas, and they allocate resources and manage time and space in ways that support teachers' work. Importantly, they recognise that leadership is not the prerogative of any one person. The defining feature of a school leader's role is the ability to mobilise the collective capacity of staff. The key element in this feature is to encourage leadership in others:

Ultimately, your leadership in a culture of change will be judged as effective or ineffective not by who you are as leaders, but by what leadership you produce in others.

Tortoises, start your engines!

(Fullan 2000 p. 137)

Part II

John Fleming

This section of the book focuses on the remarkable transformation that took place at Bellfield Primary School under the leadership of the author. John Fleming was Assistant Principal at Bellfield Primary from 1992 to 1995 and Principal from 1996 until 2005. In 2006 he became the Head of Precinct at Haileybury College in Berwick, which is known as Edrington.

1

Introduction

I have used the actual action plans, discussion papers, professional development plans, submissions, curriculum plans, mentoring program plans, strategies, recommendations, staff performance and development plans, school reviews and leadership team agendas used at Bellfield Primary School and Haileybury College to help illustrate the processes involved. I hope that these will be useful resources for those interested in the professional learning and development journey.

I have also included commentary on many initiatives, several of which proved highly successful. The concepts expressed in the Four Pillars and Three Imperatives are unique to these schools. I developed them as useful strategies to implement whole-school approaches to curriculum and student welfare.

2

Setting the scene: Bellfield Primary School 1992–2005

Bellfield Primary School is a Victorian government school servicing a low socioeconomic area in the inner northern suburbs of Melbourne. A significant section of the community is characterised by having issues with drugs, alcohol, gambling and solving problems with aggression. Employment rates are low.

I arrived at Bellfield Primary School in 1992 as the locally selected Assistant Principal. In 1991 staff morale had been so poor that Department of Education counsellors had been deployed to support the staff. There was a high turnover of teachers at the school but the staff was dedicated and hard working. They certainly had a great affection for the students at the school.

My first impressions were of a run-down school in terms of facilities and staff battling hard to support the children and the community to the best of their abilities. Student achievement was low and student welfare and student management issues needed to be dealt with. Students regularly stood up to teachers and challenged their authority. Yard duty was a daunting challenge as there were many arguments and fights. Student numbers had been declining and in 1992 were in the mid-140s.

I became the locally selected Principal in 1996 after being Acting Principal from mid-1995. Census data from 1996 revealed that just over 70 per cent of the students were eligible for the Educational Maintenance Allowance, 37 per cent of the students came from single-parent families and the proportion of students from non-English-speaking backgrounds was around 15 per cent.

Over the next 10 years these figures grew considerably. The level of disadvantage as measured by the Census rose consistently. By 2005, 85 per cent of students were receiving the Educational Maintenance Allowance, 63 per cent came from single-parent families and the students from non-English-speaking backgrounds made up around 25% of the total student population. Many of these students were refugees from Somalia with no English language background at all. There was also a significant Aboriginal population of between 15 and 20 students.

In 1992 there was, in my opinion, a Deficit Model in operation at Bellfield. Excuses were made for the poor behaviour and academic performance of the students. The students came from such disadvantaged backgrounds that it was exceptionally difficult to teach them. The teachers' attitude was 'If we get them to school on a regular basis then we are doing a good job'.

The staff believed that the top third of the students were doing well, the middle third were average and the lower third of students were struggling. The teachers were close-knit and supported each other effectively. They gained great satisfaction from supporting the children.

The school had emphasised literacy acquisition as a major school goal for several years. An early intervention literacy program known as Literacy Links had been operating at the school for a number of years. Several other schools had also adopted this program. Smaller class sizes, particularly in the Junior School (Prep to Grade 3) had also been established to allow greater attention to individual student needs. Term area planning days had been held for several years with a key focus on the English planning proforma. Fortnightly area meetings were held to assist program evaluation and the sharing of ideas and expertise. Teacher awareness of the need to improve students' learning outcomes was high.

Student welfare issues were constantly highlighted as playing a part in the lack of student achievement. In 1996, 33 per cent of students at Bellfield were diagnosed by their teachers as requiring some type of intervention service.

Professional development had been a high priority. One staff member was a former district and regional curriculum consultant for English.

The curriculum was essentially based on immersion. This followed the belief that if teachers totally immersed students in language and literacy, then students would develop the skills required to become effective learners. There was very little data gathered in the school. The school very closely followed the Victorian Education Department's Keys to Life Literacy Program (which evolved into the Early Years Literacy Program).

In 1996 the Victorian Department of Education's Accountability Framework was implemented. This involved schools in gathering data and developing plans for school improvement. Students' achievements were measured against statewide benchmarks as described in the Curriculum Standards Framework. Each year schools had to analyse a range of data in an Annual Report. Every three years a more detailed evaluation took place (the Triennial Review). A Verifier from outside the school, with significant educational background, would review the school's findings and present a report. The Accountability Framework was a very clear and precise tool for schools. It was exactly the process required to generate change at Bellfield.

The first Triennial Review for Bellfield was completed in 1996, covering the years from 1993 to 1995. The data supported my belief that the student population at Bellfield was significantly underachieving. Around 85 per cent of the students were below statewide Benchmarks in both literacy and numeracy. Most of these were well below the required performance across all grade levels from Prep to Grade 6. This was exactly what I had expected. Our review was honest and did not make excuses for poor student performance.

I prepared the parent School Council representative for the findings. She was understanding and realised that to improve student learning we needed to review our expectations and the way our curriculum was delivered to the students.

The External Verifier was pleasantly surprised by our honesty and our desire to make a difference to the student achievement levels. He was very supportive and helpful in analysing our data and for suggesting improvements. He presented to us research and programs from around the world. One such program was Robert Slavin's Success for All (1996) which would have a profound impact on our school. We also looked at Direct Instruction programs but these were certainly frowned upon by the curriculum consultants at the time.

The verification report for our Triennial Review noted the children's poor results and discussed, at length, possible strategies that would lead to improved student outcomes. Before specifically concentrating on the programs at Bellfield Primary School, the panel (myself, the School Council President and a teacher representative) discussed the international research concerning efforts to improve learning outcomes for primary students including strategies for students from disadvantaged backgrounds. The panel noted three common components in the international research projects that had been successful.

First, there had been a move away from deterministic or deficit models to models of high expectations and excellence. There had been a general view that students from disadvantaged backgrounds had had fewer opportunities to experience the 'richness of life' and that because of this 'deficit', less should be expected of them. Commonly, programs were adopted to 'broaden the horizons' of these students and poor standards were accepted on the grounds that little else should be expected from students who started so far behind the rest. The more recent models of high expectations and excellence centre on the view that all students should be expected to perform at the highest level of which they are capable. When students are expected to produce high-quality work, they usually do, irrespective of their background.

The second common component present in successful attempts to improve primary student outcomes has been the adoption of one-on-one early intervention programs.

The third common characteristic is what best can be called a holistic approach as typified by Robert Slavin's Success For All Program. Slavin's motto is that a school should do whatever it takes to generate successful outcomes for all students. The base component of Slavin's approach is a regular, high-quality literacy-teaching program that is highly structured. Activities are planned to achieve specific outcomes and little time is wasted on 'busy work'. Slavin's programs placed a high emphasis on phonics. Keys to Life was very heavily influenced by Success For All but a more eclectic approach was adopted in Victoria that blended a mixture of whole language, phonetics and other literacy paradigm approaches, in the hope of yielding large improvements in student learning.

Having discussed the international literature, the review panel returned specifically to what Bellfield could do to improve student learning. The review panel noted the large number of positive factors already in place at the school. Bellfield had already undertaken an extensive review of the Curriculum Standards Framework and the Course Advice; the Junior School teachers were involved in the Keys to Life Pilot Program; an early intervention literacy program already operated; and curriculum planning was well established.

The panel formulated the following questions:

- Are the school's expectations of the students high enough?
- Could the teaching and learning strategies used by teachers be more effective?

Bellfield Primary would now commence the journey for school improvement.

When presented with the data the staff was stunned. They realised that the more capable students at Bellfield were in fact performing very poorly when compared to statewide and 'Like Schools' benchmarks.

School improvement

Curriculum delivery

In response to the Triennial Review, I wrote a discussion paper with the title 'Making a Difference' reflecting on the major issues identified in the review and also in the verification report. The implications for our literacy program were clearly detailed. We needed:

- a balanced literacy program incorporating specific phonemic awareness activities
- regular assessment and evaluation (every five weeks) of student progress
- restructuring to provide more teaching staff for literacy sessions
- one-on one intervention incorporated into our literacy programs
- high expectations for all students.

The paper pointed to the need for substantial change to curriculum planning, delivery and evaluation. A more formal curriculum was required with an emphasis on quiet work routines and keeping on task. It would incorporate regular assessment of core literacy expectations from Prep to Grade 6 based on a balance of phonological skills and contextual learning strategies. There would be specific expectations in literacy for every grade level and all children (except those with a learning disability) would be expected to reach those levels. Children diagnosed with a learning disability would be referred to the Student Support Group and specific programs would be developed to meet their needs. Individual learning plans for all children would be devised with a special emphasis on the more capable students, to ensure that the curriculum was extending them and meeting their specific needs. The leadership team (myself, the Assistant Principal and the Leading Teacher) would play a key role in monitoring these processes. These issues were discussed at length at staff and leadership meetings. The leadership team developed sample individual learning plans and teachers were then supported in developing their own plans for specific students.

A Leadership Perspectives paper was then developed. It was to the point. The current literacy approach was not producing satisfactory results: 85 per cent of our students were below state expectations.

A Making a Difference action plan was developed. It focused on the qualities mentioned in the School Review Pilot Program: An Evaluation published by the Department of Education's Office of School Review. It highlighted the five characteristics that are repeatedly found in the literature regarding high achievement in literacy education. They were

- strong educational leadership
- high expectations of student achievement
- an emphasis on time on task
- a safe and orderly environment
- frequent evaluation of student progress.

A set of goals was designed to give clear direction to the staff. It contained the points shown in the box.

Givens
- High levels of presentation for all work
- Correction of all work
- Repeating of work not up to standard
- Work routines to be constantly emphasised and reinforced: for example, Handwriting requires a daily emphasis but should be formally taught, that is, letter formations at least three times weekly Prep to Grade 4. This should be a quiet time.

Prime Objective of Bellfield Primary School
- To improve student learning outcomes
- The **challenge** for all teachers is to work towards continuous academic improvement for all children that is **measurable**. We should not be satisfied with the status quo.

Key Question
Would I be satisfied with these standards for my own children?

The direction I wanted to take at Bellfield in terms of curriculum delivery was quite clear. I developed 'Four Pillars' to guide my direction for leading school improvement.

1   Teacher-directed learning
2   Explicit instruction
3   Moving student learning from short-term to long-term memory
4   Effective relationships between teachers and students

These Pillars would become the backbone of school improvement at Bellfield for the next decade.

The Four Pillars

Teacher-directed learning

This Pillar was important as it clearly states the position that teachers need to direct and be accountable for student learning. 'We are reclaiming teaching for teachers', I would often say. The leadership team set minimum standards in both literacy and numeracy at each grade level so that we could ensure that teachers had rigorous expectations of all students. The data for each student was reviewed term by term. The progress of all students was monitored with particular emphasis on both the struggling learners and the brighter students. For a Grade 3 student I was able to view term-by-term data from when the child had started in Prep. All teachers understood the requirement that we were expecting all children to reach our benchmarks. We wanted to replace 'happy' statements made by teachers based on perceptions with analysis of hard data.

Explicit instruction

The use of immersion teaching strategies was very evident when I arrived at Bellfield. Coupled with the mistaken strategy of student-centred learning, it was simply not producing the required results for the students. The children needed to be taught the skills of literacy and numeracy. They needed to be taken, step by step, through the learning continuums.

Learning continuums track key learning stages in the development of students' understanding of a concept. They are useful because they are not grade-based, unlike most curriculum documents. Learning continuums were beneficial at Bellfield, as we wanted to move away from grade-based learning expectations of students. Continuums enabled our brighter students to reach their academic potential more effectively. They also assisted teachers in delivering programs to meet the needs of a wide range of abilities within the one class.

Clear and explicit instruction for all students was necessary. Our teachers needed to be trained in explicit techniques via a sequential professional development program for this to occur.

Moving student learning from short-term to long-term memory

In all my teaching practice I had learnt the importance of students retaining their learning. The difference between highly effective and less competent teachers was this important facet of instruction. Many teachers in many schools follow what I term the 'chunked' learning approach. This is where learning in specific curriculum areas is taught in concentrated blocks. For example the Grade 1 teacher will teach addition in February and will then return to it in October but the topic will need to be retaught to many students as it did not move from their short-term to long-term memories.

This phenomenon occurs in schools throughout Australia. Teachers are constantly reteaching curriculum content. This Pillar indicated to teachers the importance of revision and reinforcement in all aspects of our curriculum. These factors were to be built in to all our teaching and learning programs. It was built into all our planners. We wanted to develop true mental scaffolding for the students. Revision and reinforcement were not strategies to be shunned at Bellfield but were highly desirable. We wanted our students to retain their knowledge and build on this sequentially. The Junior School developed the 'Friday Book' concept. In a dedicated notebook, the pupils revised all their learning for the week with particular emphasis on literacy and numeracy. The need to reinforce student learning constantly was regularly emphasised at staff meetings, professional development activities and planning sessions.

Effective relationships between teachers and students

In any highly effective classroom learning environment the notion of effective relationships between teachers and students is paramount. (The staff at Bellfield had many discussions as to whether this Pillar should the first one, due to its crucial nature in the craft of teaching, but it was decided to place the focus on actual teaching strategies in our effort to improve student learning.) Staff were actively encouraged to build effective relationships will all students. They understood that a breakdown in student–teacher rapport led to control issues inside and outside the classroom. Many examples of effective strategies to gain student engagement were discussed at staff meetings. The need to build bridges with students constantly was emphasised time and time again.

One of the strengths of the school was the clearly articulated school vision provided by the Four Pillars. The Pillars described our beliefs about teaching and learning. They provided us with direction in curriculum development, professional development and teacher performance.

Making a difference

The teaching and learning practices in the school were certainly not meeting the needs of the students. Change was required. A move towards more explicit instruction was required. The 'Making a Difference' paper outlined the significant changes to curriculum planning, delivery and evaluation at Bellfield.

A statement about 'Making a Difference' was released to the staff in May 1996. It began:

> Analysis of our Student Achievement results is of grave concern to me as Principal. Too many of our children are under-achieving. We need to thoroughly review our curriculum delivery, not just in English and Mathematics but in all Key Learning Areas. Teachers need to refer carefully to the Making a Difference document which outlines where we are heading.

Action plans in literacy, numeracy and student welfare were developed. These were brief and precise and clearly supported by all staff. In literacy, the school needed to improve the students' reading strategies, paying particular attention to their decoding and recoding skills. We also needed to reduce the size of our instructional groups. Focused and consistent professional development for all teachers was defined and implemented on a weekly basis to support staff.

These action plans defined our pathways to student improvement. In monitoring performance, it was agreed that we needed to be data rich. We needed to benchmark every student, every grade level and the whole school in terms of literacy and numeracy achievement. We decided to use the ACER literacy and numeracy progress tests to measure our student performance. We defined clear minimum standards for all students at each grade level, initially known as whole-school learning outcomes. Teachers were accountable for all students achieving these minimum standards in literacy and numeracy. Bellfield began to use, on a regular basis, the services of an outside consultant, Dr John Munro from the University of Melbourne, who had particular expertise in working with literacy and numeracy programs across all school levels. Data was assessed and evaluated on a term-by-term basis by the leadership team. Children who fell behind were quickly identified and strategies developed to ensure they reached acceptable standards.

The culture of the school was changed to one of student success. Staff were made accountable through annual performance reviews for their students' learning. All this was to develop in a climate of trust and respect. We were all working towards the same goals together.

Action plans were used strategically to generate curriculum and cultural change at Bellfield on a regular basis during the next five years.

Staff were regularly supported with documentation regarding aspects of our curriculum delivery. The documentation was always specific. It was designed to generate consistency throughout the school in terms of approach and implementation.

Area implementation plans started in 1999. These documents were originally designed to ensure that all staff were following the Bellfield curriculum. In time they also became a very useful resource for new staff. They outlined our teaching and learning strategies for all the key learning areas. For example, the English implementation plan in the Junior School contained sections on the Literacy Block, Reading, Fitzroy Reading Program, Shared Reading, Reading Recovery, Home Reading, Writing, Speaking and Listening, Phonemic Awareness and Handwriting. It detailed the structure of lessons and the relevant teaching strategies. This document was used to ensure consistency of approach across the school.

Student welfare

At the same time that we were reviewing curriculum delivery at Bellfield, we also reviewed the issue of student welfare. The school had been using Canter's Assertive Discipline model with only limited success. In general, the student climate in the school was not supportive of effective learning routines. Many children were constantly disrupting teaching sessions and were not motivated to learn. A vast majority were failing academically. School therefore held little worth to these students. Outside, during recesses, there were regular arguments and fights. Many students were openly defiant of the school rules and teacher directions. Peer pressure supported this disruptive behaviour.

The entire staff reviewed the Canter model and studied his tapes. We agreed that the Canter model needed to be refined. A Code of Conduct Review action plan was developed. It focused on keeping rules simple. It was decided that three rules (shown in the box) would adequately cover all situations.

---

1   Follow teacher instructions immediately.
2   Keep hands, feet and objects to yourself.
3   No calling out.

The three rules were to be applied consistently across the school. We needed to make the students accountable for their behaviour and actions. Soon after I became Principal, we devoted a series of staff meetings to student behaviour. The need for consistency of implementation was emphasised. Consequences for students who breached the rules were to be applied uniformly across all grades. The consequences took the form of three warnings: first warning (name written on the board); second warning (five minutes in at the next recess); and final warning (student sent to the Principal). I have always had a firm belief, in line with Canter, that all children given the right circumstances and environment can behave appropriately. Student behaviour certainly has an impact on their learning. School improvement at Bellfield needed to be two-pronged:

- a change in the delivery of curriculum
- a student management review to provide the necessary changes in student behaviour to maximise learning opportunities.

To engage students at school I had developed a set of Three Imperatives to assist in our student management (see box). My previous experiences as a teacher in disadvantaged schools had led me to this model.

The Three Imperatives

To be successful at school students require

- a teacher whom they believes cares for and supports them in their learning
- work at their level
- friends at school.

The Three Imperatives

A teacher whom students believe cares for and supports them in their learning

It is important for all children to feel valued. Many staff meetings were assigned to discussion focusing on the importance of the classroom environment. This environment is determined by the teacher, not the students (as many teachers believe). A firm and friendly approach to all students is essential. We emphasised the need to portray all students as good students. Labelling students was fraught with danger. We needed to highlight the good qualities of all students. This then heavily influences your perceptions and the image students believe you have of them. Students will live up to positive images just as they will live up to negative ones. It was vitally important to constantly build bridges with students. Once the bridges are knocked down, it is virtually impossible to rebuild them.

Students who do not like their teacher will consistently be issues inside and outside the classroom. An effective student management plan involves developing effective relationships with all students. The most impressive aspect of Canter's model was his understanding of this key ingredient. A student who dislikes his or her teacher will not be daunted by threats of homework, detention or the hot seat. None of these strategies will be effective because the relationship has broken down. Teachers need to demonstrate to children through actions and words that they care for them and value their feelings. They need to create an understanding and supportive environment. At Bellfield, we always emphasised that the students were the most important feature of the school. The school was there to meet their needs.

Work at their level

Many students will become disruptive and easily distracted if they perceive that the work being expected is too difficult. No one enjoys situations where they are made to feel uncomfortable but catering for the vast range of student abilities is very difficult for many teachers. At Bellfield we decided to implement whole-school structures to enable us to cater for these differences more suitably. Across the school for literacy, we decided to match student to text groups. In the Junior School, we had six classes. To reduce student numbers and to cater more adequately for the wide range of abilities, the Reading Recovery teacher also participated in Guided Reading sessions during the last 30 minutes of the two-hour literacy block. We had seven teachers. Each teacher took three groups. We had 21 teaching groups across the Junior School. The entire Junior School (Prep to Grade 3) was divided into ability groups; capable students could be grouped with older children. Instead of teachers trying to cater for a wide range of abilities, they only had to plan for three ability levels with around four to six students in each group. This also catered for the brighter students. Bright Preps could work with Grade 1 students or even Grade 2 if they were good enough. Students swapped grades for the last 30 minutes of the two-hour block.

In the Senior School we introduced an intervention group. My experience is that children prefer to work at their learning level. This enables them to progress academically at their pace. If a program has clear learning goals and these are shared with the students, then they enjoy working in small groups with other children at their level. The group was staffed by a teacher and three integration aides. Numbers were usually around 12 to 16 students, so that it was effectively a student:adult ratio of 1:3 or 4.

We first introduced learning continuums at Bellfield for this intervention group. All students were placed on a reading continuum. Teachers explained to the students where the students were in terms of their literacy skills and what skills they needed to develop. From the start this program was a great success. It engaged many children who had previously been disruptive. All students want to learn. All we have to do is open the door and they will walk through. Unfortunately, for many students the door is nearly always closed.

Friends at school

Many of the students that always appear to be in trouble at recesses are the ones with poor social skills. At Bellfield we decided to tackle this problem by aligning it with our anti-bullying strategy. The children were taught that bullying is any behaviour by another student that made them feel uncomfortable. Most of our children associated bullying with teasing and arguing or hitting and fighting. These were open forms of bullying but the often more sinister forms of bullying are more discreet. They take the form of exclusion, spreading rumours and making faces or gestures. We clearly outlined all these types of behaviours to the students at whole-school assemblies. (Assemblies were used on a regular basis to set the tone for the students in terms of work routines, code of conduct issues, work expectations and bullying.) We focused on exclusion as a means to support the pupils with poor social skills. We taught all the students at the school that exclusion was a form of bullying and that, as a team, we were all to work and play appropriately together.

Exclusion was banned. All students had to be allowed to participate in any school activity simply by asking. This included all games and activities during recesses. Over time, this proved to be an outstanding strategy. It was strictly enforced. It rapidly became an essential ingredient of our school culture. It enabled students with poorly developed social skills to participate and to make friends.

The notions of self-esteem or self worth are interesting in the context of disadvantaged schools. Many teachers are well meaning and believe the answer is to praise students on a regular basis. While this is important, it is not the key. I always emphasised to the staff at Bellfield that academic achievement was the key to success. There is no use telling the Grade 6 student who received 5 out of 20 for the mathematics test that he or she is doing well. Children will not be taken in by these sentiments. Classroom practice needs to support children to get 20 out of 20 and then they will intrinsically believe that they are worthwhile. This essential strategy was constantly reinforced at Bellfield.

Bellfield aimed to have an impact on its students' academic performance, as well as developing their social, emotional and physical abilities. This was not stated lightly; the leadership team and the entire staff focused on these issues on a regular basis. Developing students' pride in their school, their community and their country was important to us. At Monday morning whole-school assemblies, the staff and children sang the national anthem and recited the citizenship pledge. The Australian flag was raised on the flagpole every school day.

Students' respect for their teachers, their parents, adults and each other was actively encouraged, modelled and supported. For example, in the early days, staff members and I often witnessed students speaking to their parents in an inappropriate manner. We intervened and discussed this matter with both parent and student. Parents' trust in the teaching staff grew to such an extent that they would often ask us for advice and support.

Peer support was also a strong element of our school environment. All students had a 'cross-age buddy' to nurture and support. (The buddies were chosen by the respective classroom teachers after reviewing the needs of each of their students.) This was a whole-school activity and was timetabled weekly.

Leadership skills were actively taught and encouraged through the Student Representative Council, peer mediation, peer support, school captains and house captains.

Students with special needs were supported by the Student Support Group. (This strategy was recognised by the Victorian Department of Education as an effective model of good practice. It was highlighted in the Framework for Student Support Services sent to all schools in 1999.) It was a system of student case-management. The Student Support Group took referrals from school staff for any students experiencing academic, social, emotional or behaviour problems. The Principal, Student Welfare Coordinator, teacher in charge of integration, the Guidance Officer, Outreach Worker and teachers were members of the group, with outside agencies such as Berry Street and the Child Protection Society. The Student Support Group also handled referrals from parents. Individual cases were considered and an appropriate action plan developed and implemented. Regular review was a feature of the system.

The school also developed a road (traffic safety) curriculum to support the needs of its students.

Physical education and sport received a high priority and the children experienced great success at district, zone, regional and state levels. The Arts were also very strong. The school had Junior and Senior choirs, instrumental music and an annual school concert.

4

A professional learning and performance culture
Professional development

Effective professional development is an essential component of a professional learning and performance culture. It is the vehicle for improving classroom teacher practice but the challenge is to generate change in teaching strategies that teachers actually implement in the classroom. Professional development at Bellfield was always aligned to our action plans and our key learning area recommendations, which were in turn reflected in our School Charter. Teachers need to see that the professional development is relevant and achievable. It should be at the program level (as actual teaching strategies to use to implement the goals effectively) rather than the policy level (as a broad statement or set of statements about a particular curriculum area). The program level is the more effective level at which to deliver professional development as this is the level that will have more impact on classroom delivery and teacher effectiveness.

Professional development should consist of teaching strategies and activities that teachers can readily trial and evaluate. It needs to be across the board so that teachers can share their experiences and feedback to further refine their practices. Furthermore it needs to be conducted in a climate of trust and respect. It should not be judgemental or teachers will become daunted and apprehensive. Finally, it should have credibility in terms of the efficiency and ease of preparation of the activities.

In an article entitled 'School Wide Literacy Improvement Project' in *Melbourne Education* (Autumn 2001) John Munro, a regular consultant at Bellfield and participant in the school improvement process, wrote:

> Given the difficulty in bringing about, at a practical level, the type of improvement that has occurred at Bellfield, it is useful to identify the conditions seen as most influential in leading to the change.

- *A school leadership team that had a clear vision of the intended goals ...*
- *A curriculum that could lead to improvement.*
- *A professional development program approach that was based on adult learning models. It involved the following aspects:*
  1 *Staff were introduced to the concepts of phonological-orthographic knowledge and its contribution to literacy development and invited to evaluate the options and possibilities offered.*
  2 *Relevant teaching procedures were demonstrated in teachers' classes, evaluated and analysed in debriefing sessions.*
  3 *Staff worked in small action learning groups to trial, implement, evaluate and modify the teaching procedures and to integrate them with other literacy activities.*
  4 *Staff were coached individually in the implementation of the program.*
  5 *A set of integrated procedures for monitoring literacy learning progress in objective ways throughout the school. The importance of being able to track progress and to fine-tune the implementation was seen as critical. Teachers were assisted to identify and monitor indicators of literacy growth. The school uses a range of formal and informal literacy monitoring procedures.*
  6 *On-going debriefing, monitoring, tracking and planning took place at departmental and whole school levels.*

. . . The Bellfield experience identifies one set of conditions for generating sustained literacy improvement for all. Implicit in the vision are the beliefs that students can improve their literacy, that improving literacy knowledge is the responsibility of teachers in their classes and that this can happen by improving classroom teacher knowledge and teaching practice. Teachers can make a difference, particularly when they know what to do and are supported to do it.

In 1997 our Term 2 Professional Development resembled Figure 1.

We held staff meetings on a weekly basis. Rather than allocate another meeting each week to professional development (like most Victorian schools), we incorporated it into our staff meeting time. Usually 45 to 60 minutes were spent on professional development at each meeting. The use of our own teachers' expertise was constantly at the forefront. I wanted to maintain our focus on the Four Pillars and our Givens. I also wanted to demonstrate actively that our own teachers had outstanding practice and to share this amongst all our teachers. The only outside consultant used was John Munro.

We used Dr John Munro from 1997 as a consultant to great effect in our professional development program. The results were seen in the dramatic improvement in student achievement. This was supported by

---

Professional Development—Term 2 1997

The following issues will need to be addressed:

- Mathematics School Learning Outcomes
- Keys to Life/Success For All/ Other Programs
- Core Curriculum
- Specific Whole-School Learning Outcomes for work routines, homework, home reading, number, etc.
- Evaluation/Assessment
- School restructuring
- Expectations
- Code of Conduct issues
- Early Intervention/Literacy Links
- Handwriting
- Consideration of relevant research
- Development of relevant core curricula teaching/learning strategies

---

Figure 1   Sample of professional development from Bellfield Primary School

Reading Progress Tests, Statewide Testing results (LAP), the Early Years Observation Surveys and the school's Curriculum Standards Framework results. All were consistent and showed that predominantly throughout the school the children were now well above 'like schools' and at or above statewide benchmarks in literacy achievement. This information was all carefully documented in our 1999 Triennial Review and supported by our Verification Report. Our Verifier stated that the improvement in student performance was 'staggering'.

This model of professional development was used on a regular basis right through until 2005 with stunning results. Teacher classroom practice improved considerably alongside rapid increases in student achievement.

To further support our professional development program, we developed term professional development planners. These were based on our annual key curriculum area recommendations. These recommendations were based on the annual curriculum reviews (known as 'June Evaluations') undertaken by staff. These were in turn guided by our School Charter, a statement of our school goals, plans for school curriculum improvement and a description of how school improvement was to be measured. The School Charter had an overriding influence over all our planning and professional development.

The key curriculum area recommendations (Appendix 5) were a valuable tool in formulating the professional development program from year to year. They included major recommendations, overall recommendations and a section for each curriculum area.

Case study 1: Professional development

Bellfield Primary School—Barbara Alkemade, Linda Veleski, Mary Verri and Rikki Lee

There was a feeling of apprehension at first from staff members at Bellfield P.S. with the new PD plan. Staff perceived many of the ideas introduced as challenging, in that while based on research, they did not all conform to current pedagogy: for example, the use of flashcards and the emphasis on silent working sessions. These aspects were very much at odds with the teaching that was currently in place at the time. A few staff embraced the changes, particularly the staff that had been at Bellfield P.S. for some time and already had built trust and a strong rapport with the management team. Some other longer-term teachers from Bellfield were very wary about the changes. There was significant negativity, which was never discussed in front of the management team. There were traces of an underlying 'deficit model' philosophy whereby teachers felt that Bellfield children faced little hope academically because of their socioeconomic situation. Within the school, there was conflict of educational pedagogy, particularly regarding expectations and the delivery of curriculum. The whole language approach was deeply embedded within the structures of the school.

The changes to professional development actually gave teachers the skills to deliver the curriculum in a manner that would maximise student learning. As the professional development plans changed, so did the curriculum. This curriculum improved the standards of the students. The evidence that these children could succeed could not be disputed. The professional development was school-based, practical, very specific and supportive. Teachers were given clear, attainable expectations and provided with the support needed to maintain success. The development of area teams as part of the school structure ensured that teachers could discuss freely their views and concerns. Review sessions with the Principal focused intensely on the strengths of the teacher.

Dr John Munro, an expert in literacy, mathematical learning and thinking skills was employed to work with the staff very closely to develop programs to enhance student learning. Dr Munro gave professional development to the whole staff on the phonemic awareness program, mathematics planner and thinking/questioning skills that he had devised in conjunction with the staff at Bellfield.

A component of John Munro's professional development was to observe teachers in their classroom during teaching sessions. This was a source of great panic, stress and anxiousness for the Bellfield teaching staff in general. Again, our fear of the unknown was prevalent; no matter how often we were reassured that John Munro's visits were going to be a relaxed, positive experience. It is very daunting having a professor of education observing one teach and having him write copious notes: that really was incredibly unsettling.

John Munro's visits were completed in three stages. He observed each teacher for one lesson and followed this up with a 'debriefing' session where the 'copious notes' were revealed. John Munro gave genuine and positive feedback based on his observations. During the second stage, he modelled a lesson relating to the Bellfield planners. Finally, John Munro observed the classroom teacher again delivering a component of literacy they had discussed and observed Dr Munro deliver. Teachers were not passive listeners but active learners. The learning was directly applied and there was instant feedback. After two years, teachers realised there was nothing to fear and lots to be gained. As the school's results were increasingly successful, teachers' morale and enthusiasm increased.

A huge amount of professional development also came from within the school. With the strong emergence of 'team' spirit, staff shared ideas, resources and engaged endlessly in discussions about 'how to make things better'.

The changes in professional development did not happen in a vacuum. The whole curriculum changed, as did the philosophy behind it. The goal of the school was very clear and at the heart of these changes. The goal was to get our students succeeding, to have them all literate, numerate and valued. Teachers were not bogged down in the bureaucracy or politics or sidetracked by the latest PD gimmick. The professional development was a powerful tool to help the goal happen. There was an overall plan to achieve Bellfield's goal. It became a school with a clear direction and map of how to get there.

There was a shift in teacher perception of student 'ownership'. Instead of teachers looking after the interests of their grade alone, there developed a culture whereby all the children were all teachers' responsibility. The teachers and management team were united and had the same expectations for the students.

A strong message was given to the teachers about having high expectations, being kind but firm with the children. Instead of having a group of classrooms operating in isolation, where each teacher's strengths and specific culture flourished within his or her own classroom, a united whole school culture developed. The very structure of the school meant that teachers never had to plan alone. The expectations of teachers were specific and teams were set up and expected to achieve realistic goals relating to the core business—student achievement.

Haileybury College Berwick: Edrington—Gary Shiell, Jane Gibbs, Doug Bailey

Teacher performance and appraisal 2006

In 2006 Mr John Fleming introduced the Teacher Performance and Appraisal process to all staff at the Edrington precinct of Haileybury. This was in line with the whole school Professional Recognition process, but with a distinct focus on the vision for school improvement at Edrington.

Staff were familiar with the implementation of a formal PD plan, having participated in a professional recognition program over the previous three years. There was an expectation that the process would continue, but teachers were interested in any proposed changes to the system, and the impact they would have on their workload. Under the former system, staff received an individual PD allowance and obtained points for attending professional development. Selection of PD was largely self-generated, with some compulsory components, such as Dimensions of Learning (whole school) or Spelling (precinct based). Designer PD, with a membership cost of $100, was recommended as an inexpensive way of accessing a wide variety of courses throughout the year, after school hours. While this system allowed for individual choice in the selection of professional development, there were a number of associated problems. Many staff reported that they felt pressure to achieve the number of designated points necessary to fulfil the PD requirements and consequently attended courses that did not always suit their needs, or the needs of the school. Suitability of dates and venues, and attendance after school hours, also contributed to the difficulties experienced.

The Teacher Performance and Appraisal process introduced in 2006 alleviated some of these issues and was presented as a more valuable and convenient option to staff. It was clear that the school was undergoing a period of change under the direction of the new Head of Precinct, Mr John Fleming. In order to facilitate this change it was imperative that all staff develop a clear vision of the expected standards in curriculum and pedagogy. The Teacher Performance and Appraisal process was an important step towards achieving this goal. A PD template was issued to each staff member and the following differences to previous experiences were noted. Staff reacted positively to the fact that all PD requirements could be achieved on campus; that points could be obtained within the school provided that the requirements were met. This eliminated the practice of obtaining 'points for points' sake'. It was clear that the approach was closely linked to the needs of the precinct and that the PD process accommodated this. The inclusion of attendance at staff meetings and area meetings, as a component of PD, was also considered a practical element of the process by teachers, as many hours are accrued at such meetings. Staff welcomed the idea of sharing the talents of internal staff and the opportunity of working with Dr John Munro. Concerns that personal needs of teachers may not be met under this new system were discussed in the individual meetings with the Head of Precinct, and flexibility remained for staff to pursue their own interests provided the precinct requirements were met. The feedback after one year of Teacher Performance and Appraisal has been positive. The general consensus is that directions are clear and that it is easier to meet the PD requirements as set out in the new PD plans.

Performance and development culture

As described by the Victorian Department of Education and Early Childhood Development (2006), there are five key components in an effective performance and development culture:

1 induction
2 multiple sources of feedback for teacher effectiveness
3 customised individual development plans
4 quality professional development
5 teacher belief that the school has a performance and development culture.

Induction

The induction program set out to support all new teachers at the school. As Bellfield was steadily growing in student numbers, we employed new staff on a regular basis and the majority of the new teachers were graduates. The program involved three sessions for each teacher per term, consisting of interviews with me, looking at overall areas such as student expectations and the teacher's expectations and more specific areas such as actual areas of the curriculum. The sessions included evaluation of the program.

Bellfield has been innovative in delivering its induction program (Appendix 2) for many years. The program had grown and evolved alongside our continuous school improvement. The initial formal program has evolved because of the strategies implemented for school improvement and the enhancement of our performance and development culture.

Bellfield had a very clear vision that was precisely recorded in specific curriculum documents. The teaching strategies at the school were well developed, accepted and effectively implemented. New teachers to the school, especially graduates and beginning teachers, did not need to focus on what to teach as it was already documented at each grade level. They could concentrate on *how* to teach. We had a structured and sequential set of curriculum programs at Bellfield in all the key learning areas.

The structure of the curriculum planning enabled teachers to develop their teaching skills and strategies effectively. This was supported by exceptionally strong professional learning teams. These teams focused on student achievement and the most effective teaching methods to attain outstanding results.

The teacher performance and development process at Bellfield focused specifically on developing the teachers' skills. It was explicit and was widely regarded as best practice. Over the years the process evolved further from just formal meetings. New teachers still met with the Principal, Assistant Principal and coordinators. Expectations and school documentation was still clarified. However this was clearly supported by our structure of staff meetings, professional development, area meetings and planning documents.

As an indication of staff morale it can be noted that in the years 1996 to 2005 no full-time Staff member at Bellfield transferred from the school, although several teachers were successful in applying for promotion.

Multiple sources of feedback for teacher effectiveness

Bellfield has been innovative in delivering multiple sources of feedback to teachers for many years. The practices were state of the art and received positive responses from a wide range of sources.

The school was data rich. AIM, RPT, NPT, CSF, P-2 Testing, TORCH, SAST, Running Records, Reading Levels and Lexiles were all used in the Teacher Performance Development and Review process. Testing was supported by specific classroom observation sessions conducted by the Principal. This was certainly one of the most effective strategies in our school improvement and in developing teachers' skills. It was specific and not based on the Department of Education's standards, which were far too broad to support individual development and subsequently school improvement.

Teachers in the Senior School (Grades 4–6) also had the opportunity to discuss and review student feedback through Student Attitudes to Schooling Surveys, POLT (Principles of Learning and Teaching) and MYPRAD Student Surveys. The leadership team analysed each teacher's student achievement data in literacy and numeracy with a view to supporting members of staff in improving student learning outcomes.

The Mentoring and Modelling Program allowed teachers to give and receive feedback after taking part in classroom visits within the school. The staff found this to be supportive and productive and was yet another opportunity to align practices and develop consistent approaches within the school.

All the procedures were based on trust and respect. These are crucial ingredients for an effective staff performance program.

Various feedback measures, including staff opinion surveys and surveys conducted by the Boston Consulting Group and held as part of an accreditation process for the Department of Education, all clearly indicated an exceptional level of support for our program.

Customised individual development plans

The staff all had individual professional development plans. These were supported by whole-school professional development plans. These evolved into key learning area recommendations. Individual professional development plans were developed at the start of each year by each teacher, in conjunction with senior staff, within school guidelines. (Initially, the teacher and I evaluated the plan during the performance management process.) The staff knew the whole-school plans and they incorporated them into their own individual professional development plans. The individual plans gave teachers the opportunity to pursue their own specific areas of interest. The entire process was then outlined in the key learning area recommendations, which were the specific teaching and learning improvements detailed for each subject area. This cycle of individual plans, school plans and key recommendations played an integral part in our school performance and development culture. It focused attention on areas for improvement and was matched with our professional development, both for individuals and the whole staff.

Individual plans were regularly monitored as part of the performance development and review program and also for our annual report. They were clearly linked to our School Charter. Staff career and leadership aspirations were also incorporated into this process.

Over a period of years, the responsibility for individual development plans was more and more handed over to the individual teacher. The plans were not strictly monitored because most of the professional development became school-based. As student achievement consequently improved dramatically, the professional development program was a success.

Quality professional development

All professional development at Bellfield was related to the Four Pillars. The delivery of professional development was strategic and not ad hoc. It was clearly focused on teaching and learning and direct classroom practice. It was delivered at the program not policy level. Our practices were precise and informative. The use of an outside consultant (John Munro) was innovative and highly successful. From 2004 all the teachers had professional learning partners. Relevant discussion and feedback were initially used to develop our mentoring program. Many schools visited Bellfield resulting in our staff providing resources and expertise to the visitors on a regular basis.

The development of learning continuums involved the entire teaching staff in highly effective professional development at the program level. The key learning area recommendations were the basis for the professional development program. These were derived from our June evaluations, annual reports, triennial reviews and from the School Charter.

As part of the professional development program, the leadership team set defined targets and expectations for individual teachers and teams of teachers.

The annual professional development strategy (Appendix 3) and professional development plan (Appendix 4) described the process for determining professional development activities for the year. Professional development was always aligned with our School Charter and Key learning area recommendations. Professional development was ongoing and consistent. It always focused on classroom practice. The performance review process was used to ensure that teachers were implementing the strategies and refining their own performance.

The school was always looking for better ways of supporting teachers in their professional learning. Our professional partners program was effective in establishing mentoring at our school. The leadership team selected the partners on the basis of equal experience and that the partners taught similar grade levels. The partners' first meeting was with the leadership team and lasted for some 90 minutes. Each partner was asked to identify an area where she or he felt able to model effective teaching practice to others. Each partner was also asked to define an area in which she or he wanted to improve. All staff, including the leadership team, were involved in the program. After the partners system had given initial impetus to the mentoring program, it had served its purpose and was discontinued. The first mentoring sessions covered several areas. The Senior School teachers concentrated on Guided Reading.

The partners system was used to highlight the need for mentoring to be non-judgemental. It was to be supportive, a means for confirming teachers' own good practices and an opportunity to witness and investigate new teaching strategies. From the start, the feedback was impressive. The staff implemented the program in a positive and supportive environment. This document (shown in Figure 2) was developed to inform staff of the process.

Partners' Professional Development 2003

Teachers have all been allocated partners as an enhancement to our regular Professional Development activities.

These partners will spend time with our Curriculum Coordinators—John, Heather and Maree—in assisting us to improve our school programs. The purpose will be to review and refine our current curriculum in terms of content and delivery in all subject areas. This is as a response to the improved student performance throughout the school at all grade levels. We need to ensure our teaching and learning strategies continue to cater for all our students in the best possible manner.

We will be reviewing all areas of our school including timetabling and appropriate use of resources.

We will also be exploring the opportunities for teacher modelling of effective teaching strategies throughout the school.

Teachers are asked to prepare the following beforehand:
* Bring samples of student work in all subject areas
* List all the positive aspects of your teaching
* List any areas you feel you require support or further learning.

Figure 2   Information for staff about the partners' professional development program at Bellfield

Case study 2: Partners' professional development program

Bellfield Primary School—Linda Veleski and Rikki Lee

The management team, which included the Principal, Vice Principal and team leader, were responsible for the running of the partners' professional development program. All teachers were interviewed, initially with partners. We were interviewed for approximately an hour and a half, and we discussed our own areas of teaching strengths and also areas for improvement. Teachers were encouraged to express which areas they felt comfortable in mentoring. John Fleming's approach towards this mentoring program was professional, supportive and clear. As most staff members had already experienced other forms of mentoring with John Munro, the majority of staff felt comfortable with visitors in the classroom. Younger staff were reassured that judgements were not going to be made, yet they still felt daunted about the idea. Particular individuals, who had been teaching for a number of years, felt that they would not gain knowledge from this experience. But after participating in the mentoring program, their views did change and they saw the benefits of supporting each other.

As young staff members, we found the experience to be extremely beneficial as we gained skills in many areas such as student management, time management and curriculum delivery. Questioning of students during guided reading tasks was also an area we gained more experience in after the mentoring sessions were completed. Younger staff began to feel reassured that they were teaching the curriculum correctly and using effective teacher practice. Overall staff felt valued, confident and united as a team at the completion of the mentoring program.

Term-by-term professional development plans supported our whole-school plan and the key learning area recommendations. These professional development planners ensured our program was not ad hoc. We did not simply fill in dates with activities. It was carefully planned and purposeful. It was ongoing and consistent. We used the same consultant for more than 10 years to provide continuity and development. There were common themes from year to year.

Teacher belief that the school has a performance and development culture

Various surveys, including annual staff surveys and one conducted by the Boston Consulting Group, all indicated a strong staff belief in the effectiveness of our performance and development culture. The Boston survey in particular demonstrated just how highly staff felt about the school. (The work at Bellfield informed Boston Group's report on school improvement for the Education Minister, which subsequently became the Blueprint for Education in Victoria.)

Student achievement was always our core business. It was constantly highlighted and discussed. Staff took great pride in the continual improvement of our student achievement data.

Key aspects of school improvement at Bellfield included

- **team planning**: this occurred at area meetings on a fortnightly basis with a major emphasis on curriculum delivery. We had specific curriculum planners in every key learning area.
- **planning days**: these were held once a term to enable our teaching teams to discuss and review the curriculum delivery for the next term.

- **curriculum days**: consistent with government guidelines these were held four times a year. They were used for professional development to support our whole-school professional development plans.
- **term professional development**: staff meetings usually had a professional development focus.

The importance of explicit instruction for students and the pace of that instruction was constantly reinforced and modelled at Bellfield. The pace or intensity of instruction was a key component of our curriculum improvement. In order to incorporate all the specific learning skills required to enhance students' progress, teachers need to plan their delivery carefully. It needs to be teacher-intensive and students have to be trained to focus their attention. This does not just simply occur. Teachers need to be specifically trained to develop this skill. When I visited classrooms, I always closely monitored students' focus. I regularly provided individual feedback to teachers with specific recommendations on how they could improve their practice. To deliver a comprehensive curriculum in literacy and numeracy, teachers have to be time efficient in the implementation of that program.

Case study 3: A customised individual development plan

Haileybury College, Berwick: Edrington—Gary Shiell, Jane Gibbs, Doug Bailey

With the implementation of the Teacher Performance and Appraisal plan teachers were provided with a clear outline of what was expected from them throughout the course of the year. This included the following five areas: Professional Recognition Program (PRP) interview, classroom visits, interview/feedback, formal documentation and professional development (PD)/mentoring. The aims of this plan were

- to improve teacher practice, that is, to build teacher capacity
- to enhance teacher career and leadership skills
- to support curriculum development at the school

A PD template (shown Figure 3) was distributed to each member of staff, indicating the requirements for the year. The plan was divided into two sections: Professional Development Activities and Special Interest PD. The Professional Development Activities, in the initial stages of this process, tended to be controlled by John Fleming, directed towards the whole precinct focus, while the Special Interest component allowed for the individual needs of each teacher to be considered. There was some concern that PD plans were not individual enough and that PD budgets would not be available under the new system. Staff met with their relevant Head of School to discuss both the compulsory section related to the new direction of the school, and to negotiate any extra PD they might express interest in. Individual PD plans were then developed and submitted to John. Whilst the precinct focus was non-negotiable, teachers' individual needs were elicited by observation of performance and personal requests.

**HAILEYBURY COLLEGE—BERWICK
PROFESSIONAL DEVELOPMENT PLAN 2006**

NAME:

Professional Development Activities
Staff meetings—whole-school PD
Area meetings—implementation of new directions in curriculum
- Development of new planners
- Sharing good practice
Involvement in mentor program
Classroom visits program and feedback
Professional recognition program—documentation and
   interview
Off-campus Staff Conference
ICT

Special Interest PD
VELS Reporting
Habits of Mind
First Aid

Figure 3   Sample PD template of individual teacher's plan at
Haileybury College

Teacher performance

Closely aligned to school improvement and professional development was the staff performance program. This started in 1996. It followed the Victorian Education Department's model of staff appraisal with a number of key differences. The model used a set of teaching standards to review staff performance. The cycle was for a period of one year. It involved a series of interviews with the Principal. An introductory interview was held to discuss the standards and ensure that all staff were familiar with them. This was followed by a mid-cycle interview to review progress and to highlight any shortcomings. At the end of the cycle, a final interview determined the teacher's overall performance for the year. This process was obligatory for all staff. Many schools simply were compliant with this process and never really used the opportunity to develop and enhance teacher classroom practice but I found this to be the ideal vehicle to support Bellfield's school improvement agenda. The most important factor in raising student achievement is the skills of the classroom teachers.

I wanted to make sure the process had credibility with the teachers. The only way to do this was to actually watch the teachers teach, so as to provide real feedback on their performance. It was also a highly effective means of ensuring the school expectations were being met. The observation sessions proved to be a significant means of building teacher capacity. It was always stressed that just as continuous improvement was an important ingredient in any high performing school, so was individual teacher continuous improvement. This process, especially the teacher observation sessions, was the critical difference between the Bellfield teacher performance model and that of other schools.

Case study 4: The idea of observation

Bellfield Primary School—Barbara Alkemade,
Linda Veleski, Mary Verri and Rikki Lee

Initially, when John Fleming introduced classroom visits, he was the only person conducting the formal observations. The whole idea of the Principal coming into our classrooms to observe us delivering curriculum sent 'shockwaves' through our teaching staff. Most definitely the staff feared the proposal that classroom observations were to be introduced for all teachers. The prospect of classroom visits by the Principal became the main focus of our conversation. The staff spoke amongst themselves, sharing their concerns either privately or in forums such as professional learning team meetings. Initial reactions ranged from fear through to anger that our professional integrity was being challenged. Furthermore, some of us, the more experienced teachers, felt insulted while the young teachers, particularly graduates, were truly terrified. Questions were raised as to our Principal's understanding of teaching, belief in his staff and desire to 'control' without really respecting us as teaching professionals.

We failed to see the 'big picture'. We were teaching professionals who were in this career to teach and provide every child with the opportunity to make choices now and in the future. Without being literate, numerate and social beings choices in life are very limited. To enable the children at Bellfield Primary School to have these opportunities, their learning needed to be direct and explicit with sequentially developed programs that maximised student learning outcomes. At the early stage of John Fleming's leadership at Bellfield Primary School he sought to move away from the 'deficit' model that had prevailed. His passion and drive was to undeniably demonstrate that all children, regardless of their socioeconomic status, ethnicity or home environment, can learn, given the right curriculum delivery and learning environment. John had the research to support his beliefs and the intensity and vigour to achieve success.

The outline of expectations was daunting to many members of staff. Teachers were afraid of the unknown. It was something that they were not used to and it forced teachers out of their comfort zone. After it was implemented, teachers realised that the feedback was overwhelmingly positive. The process was handled with the underlying philosophy of supporting the staff and giving them the specific skills and training for them to succeed. Areas needing improvement were dealt with on an individual level at a later date or were approached through whole-staff professional development sessions. There was no doubt that staff were somewhat relieved when the initial visit and feedback sessions were completed. This still did not alter the fact that as a group we still experienced some anxious moments when class visits were on again. We always reflected on what was happening in our classrooms in regard to the children's learning and evaluated ourselves very thoroughly, being extremely hard critics. John continued his positive approach when conducting our appraisals. He reinforced the positive aspects publicly in staff meetings, administrative meetings and at school council meetings.

Something extremely important came from this process. As a staff we openly shared our classroom techniques, successes and areas needing improvement. We came together as a team with a common goal of continual improvement, both for ourselves as educators and for our students. We supported and encouraged each other. Our school was a place of learning for the entire school community: students, teachers, parents and the wider community.

Haileybury College Berwick: Edrington—Gary Shiell, Jane Gibbs, Doug Bailey

A new initiative to the Professional Recognition Process (PRP) was the introduction of classroom visits and teacher observations. It was clear that this had the biggest impact on staff with varied reactions throughout the boys' and girls' middle schools.

The observation program required staff to have their teaching practice observed by their peers and the heads of Middle School. Each staff member was also required to observe four teaching sessions delivered by other teachers within the school. The initial reaction was generally one of shock. Many teachers did not feel comfortable with the proposal.

Concerns were expressed about how the process would be carried out and the legalities involved with such a process. Many staff felt anxious and commented that they were reminded of their student-teacher days. In general, concerns were related to performance on the day, not curriculum or planning issues. Reactions varied.

New graduates
While new graduates or inexperienced teachers were familiar with the notion of being observed during their classes, they were anxious that they would be judged on their performance and that their jobs may be at risk. They were worried that they might not reach the high standard expected.

Very experienced teachers
On the whole, these staff members were comfortable with their teaching style and took the attitude that their experience was adequate to get them through the process. While many made a special effort to plan the 'observation' lesson, others took the 'take it as it comes' attitude.

Parallel education
In general, teachers of girls' classes were less concerned about the impact of student behaviour than teachers of boys' classes were. Teachers felt that a snapshot of their teaching, where a boy might behave poorly in class, would unfairly influence the observer's opinion of their class management.

Specific subjects
Some teachers felt that if a child disliked the subject they taught (but it was compulsory for them to study it) their attitude might negatively influence the observer, despite best efforts to engage the child.

Before the start of the teacher observations, all teachers were provided with a check list (shown in Figure 4), listing the areas the observers would be focusing on during their visits. The purpose of this was to reassure staff that there was no hidden agenda and to allow them to be fully prepared.

Classroom Visits Check List

Display

Presentation

Time on task

Organisation

Tone

Student management

Planning

Lesson structure

Questioning

Use of resources

Student feedback

Student engagement

Work routines

Clarity of instructions

Correction

Expectations

Figure 4   Sample classroom visits check list, Haileybury College

In addition to the check list, a proforma was developed by the heads of Middle School, to be completed during the observation process. This included the check list and anecdotal records that would provide the basis of the feedback interview. These anecdotal records were the on-the-spot jottings of the observer and based on the check list, which all staff were familiar with.

In order for the observation process to be well received, a positive focus was maintained at all times. Staff were encouraged to select the class they wished to be observed teaching, provided that explicit teaching was evident.

Case study 5: Outcomes of observation

Haileybury College, Berwick: Edrington—Gary Shiell, Jane Gibbs, Doug Bailey

While there is no doubt that the introduction of the Teacher Observation and Classroom Visits component of the PRP process caused initial discomfort, in actuality it became a positive experience for the teachers involved. The braver teachers, who volunteered to be observed first, reported to others that it was an affirming process and the news soon spread that it was not as stressful as first imagined. Despite the fact that it was a time-consuming process, requiring the heads of Middle School to be released from their other duties, they indicated that it was a rewarding experience for all involved.

Feedback was provided on the same day, in the form of an interview and written report, provided by the heads of Middle School. Strengths were identified and areas for improvement targeted. It was noted by the observers that the teachers themselves were the harshest critics and identified their own shortcomings more readily than their good qualities. Staff reported that they enjoyed hearing positive comments about their teaching practice and that the process made them feel valued.

New graduate
This teacher was extremely anxious about the process and found the build-up to the observation session very stressful. In actual fact, her lesson was one of the best examples of explicit teaching observed. It was noted that this teacher had taken into consideration all of the

requirements as directed and her efforts had resulted in an outstanding lesson. She was encouraged by the positive feedback.

LOTE Teacher—experienced
This teacher, although very experienced, was nervous about her observation session. She admitted to preparing more thoroughly than usual, and she had included a variety of teaching styles and activities within her lesson. At the end of the session she was able to identify the more successful components of her lesson and use this knowledge to modify her future planning. She was pleased with the positive feedback and commented that it was an uplifting experience to be praised, even after all her years of experience.

On the whole, the implementation of the process was introduced as a positive experience. After the process, the staff felt more comfortable and believed it had been a worthwhile experience. The next stage in the future direction of the school has now been established and teachers are aware of what is required of them. Teaching practice has been improved in line with this and the PRP has been implemented further in 2007.

The professional recognition program followed the same basic formula over the years. The information shown in Figure 5 was distributed and discussed on the first day of each school year.

Staff were then provided with a more detailed description of the process, along with a class visits and interview timetable (shown in Figure 6).

At times, the professional development process was slightly modified to include specific reference to teachers' evaluation of their teaching strengths and areas for improvement. Teachers needed to bring these to the interview in written form. At other times, specific curriculum initiatives were targeted: for example, Bellfield's 2001 annual review highlighted general knowledge expectations, automatic response/number facts, written expression, literacy thinking skills, handwriting and home reading and these areas were then targeted in teachers' individual professional development plans as well as whole-school plans.

Each classroom visit lasted between 30 and 40 minutes. I looked at the students' workbooks to check teacher correction and feedback, presentation, handwriting and that all work was completed. I also listened to a range of children read and seek feedback from them regarding their enjoyment of school and their opinion of their learning progress. Teachers were invited to leave out for show any student work that they were

Staff Performance and Development Arrangements 2005
These areas will form the basis of the interviews:
- Expectations of students
- Commitment to team/ Professional approach
- Literacy
- Numeracy
- Presentation of children's work, work routines, correction, display and control
- Performance of job description
- Review of performance plans for eligible staff
- Implementation of key curriculum area major recommendations 2005

Personal Professional Development Plans
These plans will be similar to previous years with a compulsory Learning Technology section. This will be a component of all plans. These will contain specific goals and outcomes for all teachers along with achievement measures. Heather and Stephen will be available to assist with the development of professional development plans with regards to learning technologies. In addition staff will need to carefully consider outlining the evidence that will support achievement of their specific goals. If in doubt consult John.

Figure 5   Outline of staff professional development process, Bellfield Primary School

particularly pleased with. During this time, I made notes on the teacher's teaching strategies. I noted student management procedures, organisation of teaching resources, explicit instruction, questioning and the engagement of the students. For beginning teachers, often I would have about four pages of notes. After the classroom visits, I always ensured that I left with a positive comment.

The next stage was to meet with the area coordinators and write down relevant feedback. This was then presented to the staff member in an interview. I always tried to make the interviews as positive as possible. The process was about building teachers up, not knocking them down.

Staff found the process daunting until they experienced it. Once credibility and trust had been established, the teachers found the process affirming and an important part of their teaching development. They liked the specific feedback relevant to their own individual teaching practice. They embraced the system as a valuable link in an ongoing process. It enhanced the notion of continuous teacher improvement.

Staff Performance and Development 2005
- Contribution to team
- Teacher control
- Class tone
- Class work routines
- DISPLAY
- EXPECTATIONS
- CORRECTION
- PRESENTATION OF WORK
- Implementation of school literacy and numeracy programs
- Individual learning plans
- Implementation of job description

VIA
- Feedback from area coordinators
- Classroom visits
- Interviews

Teachers need to have the following available during the classroom visits and bring these documents to the interview:
- Class timetable
- Work program
- Term-by-term planning proformas
- Evaluation and assessment records
- Personal professional development plans
- Area implementation plans
- Any other relevant material

Specialist teachers will need to demonstrate the link between their programs and the relevant CSF documents and the relevance of their assessment strategies to the CSF learning outcomes.

Figure 6   Detail of staff professional development process, Bellfield
Primary School

In 2003, The Boston Consulting Group (BCG) visited Bellfield as part of the design of the Schools Workforce Development Strategy for Victorian government schools. Staff were interviewed, participated in focus groups and surveyed online regarding workforce development practices and issues at the school. In an email to me, Kate Cotter (of BCG) wrote:

We are collecting examples of excellent practice from the school visits that we have conducted and I would like to include Bellfield PS on several dimensions:
- *Shared vision and leadership to bring about change*
- *Constructive feedback to staff through observation*
- *Approach to recognition of staff*

BCG's findings in these areas at Bellfield were:

Bringing about change:
- *School leaders established a clear and simple vision for what the school and teachers want to achieve—a vision shared by staff*
- *School leaders set the culture and clear expectations about what will be achieved and how staff will work together to do this*
- *School leaders demonstrate confidence in the staff to achieve the vision, providing encouragement and support*
- *The vision and plan are linked to manageable goals and targets. While the overall plan has a long-term time frame, specific strategies are in place that define manageable steps for achieving the goals. For example, in the first year of the plan teachers focused on improving outcomes in reading and writing, rather than across the entire curriculum. This particular strategy relieved pressure on staff and legitimised the focus on priority areas*

Constructive feedback to staff:
- *The principal understands the importance of constructive feedback in encouraging staff and helping them to improve. There are three key aspects to this:*
  - *Feedback balances positive aspects with areas for improvement. School leaders recognise the need to encourage and build confidence, rather than simply criticise*
  - *The school leaders are able to model excellent teaching (i.e., demonstrate what should happen in the classroom)*
  - *The principal invests time in giving constructive feedback to staff. Feedback through observation is an essential element. He visits classrooms, observes teaching and examines the students' work. The observation allows the principal to give rich constructive feedback and tailored suggestions on how teachers can address specific challenges. It also enables him to encourage staff and reinforce areas of strength. In our focus groups and interviews, staff reported that they initially found this confronting but now find it worthwhile and non-threatening, since it is not punitive but constructive*

Approach to recognition:
- *School leaders provide recognition of individual staff members in private discussions, for example, giving positive feedback, encouragement and specific examples of the impact that their teaching is having on students*
- *In staff meetings, the principal/school leaders recognise the effort and work of individual teachers and teaching teams that improve the learning outcomes for Bellfield students and help the school to realise its vision*

- *School leaders also celebrate successes and progress towards the school's goals with the school community and the public, for example, winning the Herald Sun School of the Year Award in 2000*

Boston Consulting provided the school with a report ('Engaging for Results', 29 July 2003), which included our own online results, and comparisons with the other schools surveyed. A rating scale of 1.0 to 5.0 was used: scores of between 1.0 and 3.2 revealed areas of weakness; 3.2 to 3.8 improvement opportunities; and 3.8 to 5.0 indicated strong performance.

The overall results for Bellfield Primary were

Performance disciplines 4.8

Collective commitment to objectives 4.9

Sharp individual accountabilities 4.9

Rigorous performance management 4.8

Platforms for collaboration 4.7

Capable workforce 4.8

Personal motivators 4.8

Shared vision, values, pride 4.8

Empowerment 4.7

Recognition and appreciation 4.8

Supportive environment 4.7

Pathways for personal growth 4.7

Overall satisfaction 4.9

Leadership 4.9

Communication 4.7

Bellfield recorded the highest scores in all surveyed areas of all the surveyed schools.

The performance management system at Bellfield not only supported individual teacher growth but also allowed for the monitoring of school programs and the implementation of new initiatives. It made teachers accountable for their own performance. It encouraged and supported teachers in their quest to be better teachers. It was always informed by data. Individual, class and grade level student progress was monitored on a regular basis. While this information was not formally used as part of the review process, the leadership team considered the information before the review process. As student progress was always on the increase, it was not deemed appropriate to use the information individually but the information was collected and evaluated by the leadership team on a term-by-term basis.

In 2005 Bellfield became one of the first group of schools to be accredited as a school with a performance and development culture as part of the government's new Blueprint for Education. The Australian Council *for* Educational Research's Accreditation Report noted:

Bellfield Primary School has established a performance and development culture which was clearly confirmed by the school visit. The school has also received a number of individual and whole school awards which indicate this culture has been achieved.

While the school does currently have new teachers, it has in place a comprehensive and effective induction program which has been developed over a number of years.

Many sources of feedback are used to improve teacher effectiveness at Bellfield. These include multiple sources of student data and student surveys. Student data is rigorously collected and analysed. A mentoring and modelling program to give teachers feedback after classroom visits was established several years ago, and the interviewer was able to see documents cited in the application that confirm the success of the feedback process. As in other areas, the Performance and Development Culture Questionnaire (PDCQ) data is strong.

All staff interviewed were able to articulate the school's development procedures and practices. They were able to talk about the range of methods and feedback they were offered in the school and to reflect on how this helped them to improve student learning outcomes.

Teachers also spoke impressively about the activities that were incorporated into their individual professional development plans and their school-wide professional learning. They showed a clear understanding of how their own classroom practice needed to be linked to whole school practice in order to maximise student learning. The school provides an extensive range of professional development opportunities.

The extensive recognition which Bellfield has received in the wider educational community is very impressive. The interviewer saw a range of convincing evidence... The school has engaged students in a learning program that is explicit, challenging and particularly effective in raising student learning outcomes. The PDCQ and other data, together with the school visit, convincingly confirm that Bellfield is a school with a high level of perform-ance and development culture that has been developed over a number of years and that is being shared in the wider educational community.

Future Directions

The school may be able to play a major role in demonstrating innovative programs and procedures and their positive impact on teaching and learn-ing. The further development and explication of measures of effectiveness should assist in this regard, as should a clear and comprehensive presentation of the school's current progress and achievements as measured against Level 5 criteria.

After accreditation, Bellfield became a 'Reference School' and supported many other schools in the accreditation process.

5

Bellfield 2005

Bellfield Primary in 2005 was a very different school from the same school in 1992. It had developed an effective culture of staff professional development. This online survey was completed by the teachers at Bellfield (full details in Appendix 6). Scores were out of a total of 5 for each question.

Customised individual teacher development plans 4.7
Quality professional development 4.8
Performance and development culture 4.9

These results clearly indicated that the staff believed that the school had an effective performance and development culture. They reflect the great personal satisfaction that teachers get when they have data that shows that are making a difference to student achievement and hence increasing their life chances. All teachers want to make a difference to their students but the curriculum must be delivered effectively. All elements of the school need to be geared towards the goal of student achievement. Success comes via careful planning. It does not just happen. Effective practice in monitoring and improving teacher performance is integral to this success.

As a consequence of this effective culture, Bellfield had developed a very effective student culture of learning and social development and it had succeeded in raising the level of student achievement across the board. There have been many indicators of the school's success.

Bellfield data

ACER Testing

Reading Progress Test

A score of 100 indicates that a student's reading level matches their chronological age. Bellfield benchmarked every student, every grade level and the whole school.

Whole-school scores:

1997	92.7
1998	93.7
1999	95.19
2000	98.67
2001	106
2002	104
2003	111
2004	116

Numeracy Progress Test

Whole-school scores:

2001	106
2002	108
2003	116
2004	115

Victorian statewide Prep–2 Testing 2004

Prep—reading with 100 per cent accuracy at level 1
  Bellfield 96% (1998 result 33.3%)
  Like Schools Group 57.1%
  Statewide 67.2%

Grade 1—reading with 100% accuracy at level 15
  Bellfield 98% (1998 result 34.6%)
  Like Schools Group 28.9%
  Statewide 36.4%

Grade 2—reading with 100% accuracy at level 20
  Bellfield 91% (1998 result 30.6%)
  Like Schools Group 39%
  Statewide 47.7%

Other measures

Curriculum Standards Framework Results

CSF results indicated that Bellfield students at all grade levels performed at the top of the state in literacy and numeracy.

Awards

The school has won many awards over the past few years. Bellfield won the *Herald Sun* Teacher Team of the Year Award in 2000. The Principal was a finalist in the *Herald Sun* Principal of the Year Award in 2003. The school also won state and national literacy and numeracy awards in 2000 and 2003. In 2003 we received a High Commendation for our literacy and numeracy programs in the National Quality Schools Awards. In 2003 the Principal received an award for Educational Leadership from the Australian College of Educational Leadership. In 2005 the Principal was a finalist in the Education Excellence Awards for School Leadership.

Student opinion

Student opinion survey results indicated that the school is in the top 10 per cent of schools in all areas measured.

Parent opinion

The statewide Parent Opinion Surveys have for many years shown that Bellfield was substantially above statewide benchmarks in most areas surveyed.

Visitors and presentations

Over the past few years Bellfield has welcomed many visitors. The Principal has also presented the Bellfield school improvement model throughout the state. Bellfield has been in high demand as a school that provides an effective model for school improvement.

In 2005 the deputy secretary for education in Victoria, Darrell Fraser, visited Bellfield. In his statewide *Principals Newsletter* he stated:

> *John Fleming, the Principal of Bellfield, is a passionate educator with a clear vision for his learning community and a staff committed to their students and to their own professional growth as educators. It was a wonderful opportunity to interact with students and staff and to witness the level of engagement that has resulted from purposeful teaching and a belief in the capacity and potential of all their students to engage with challenging content.*

In a letter to me as Principal he stated:

> *I was particularly impressed with the school's educative vision through its four pillars and the understanding of the factors that support an effective learning community . . . Your professional learning agenda has enabled all your staff to develop their understanding of the teaching and learning process and the conditions that support it.*

6

Some thoughts on leadership

Leadership is a key ingredient in school improvement and the establishment of a professional learning and development culture. The nature of leadership was regularly discussed at Bellfield so that all staff had a clear understanding.

Building the leadership capacity of teachers is an essential component of any educational organisation. Effective leadership needs to be modelled. Leadership is about being involved in school planning, professional development and general school activities. It is about showing that the effective delivery of curriculum is the key school focus. In my mind, the shuffling of papers in the Principal's Office never supported the development of student achievement that is education's core business. The Principal needs to lead curriculum development rather than focus on the administration of the school. Administration is important but it is not the school's core business.

There are three important characteristics I have found to be very useful: passion, determination and vision.

Passion

The entire staff needs to witness your passion for education and your desire for school improvement. It needs to be apparent and a key part of guiding the whole school.

Determination

The entire staff needs to witness your determination that the processes implemented will make a difference and that you can achieve your goals as a school. The staff needs to be influenced by consistency and a well-planned approach.

Vision

A regular feature of my time at Bellfield was reinforcing the vision that was so essential to our success. A vision needs to be clear and precise. Overall school statements that talk about excellence for all students are often just meaningless words unsupported by effective processes and practices. A vision needs to be a clear statement on teaching and learning. The Four Pillars were developed to meet this need for clarity and unity of purpose. A vision needs to be constantly reinforced. It needs to live in the minds of the staff.

An extremely important aspect of leadership is the balance between work and family life. My family always comes first. This is the culture I have endeavoured to establish at both Bellfield and Haileybury. The balance between work and home is crucial in establishing a healthy workplace environment.

The key aspects for leadership in my opinion are

- **vision**: described by the Four Pillars
- **pedagogy**: the implementation of the Four Pillars
- **practice**: the effectiveness of teachers' instruction
- **accountability**: reviewing teachers' performance in light of student achievements
- **data**: measuring and evaluating students' achievements
- **culture** (both student and teacher): the tone of the school and in particular, student management strategies.

In developing leadership skills at Bellfield and in informing staff of leadership perspectives we regularly discussed the leadership role.

Other important facets of leadership

In addition to the characteristics discussed in the previous section, there are some specific areas and actions, in my mind, that demonstrate good leadership.

Staff recruitment

Selecting the right staff is an essential component of effective school leadership. The 'get along skills' of your staff are very important. This was always a factor in staff recruitment at Bellfield. You can support a teacher in developing curriculum skills but I do not believe you can support them in caring for children. I believe this is an inherent quality of effective teachers.

Grade-based learning

Effective leadership involves setting high expectations of student performance. It also necessitates establishing curriculum delivery structures to cater for the learning needs of all students across the spectrum. I feel very strongly that our education systems and schools support grade-based learning that is, that Grade 1 work is covered in Grade 1. I also believe many Grade 1 students are capable of much more. We need to incorporate structures in our schools to allow our students to reach their potential. At Bellfield we matched all our students to text across the whole of the Junior and Senior schools. If a Grade 1 student was good enough, then she or he could work with Grade 2 or Grade 3 students.

Excellence

Skilled educational leaders develop mechanisms within their schools to promote and to model excellence in teaching practice. At Haileybury, I asked a particularly high-performing teacher to model outstanding practice for the entire staff. Permission was sought for her students to stay after school during staff meeting time. The teacher modelled outstanding explicit instruction that created much discussion among all the staff members. Many teachers have not been exposed to what I define as true excellence in teaching. They engage in 'privatism' and work within the confines of their classroom. This does not allow them to witness outstanding practice. They attend many one-off professional development activities that in the end only minimally influence classroom practice. Mentoring and coaching expose teachers to excellence. It is crucial in developing excellent teaching practices. At Edrington, each teacher is required to visit eight other classroom sessions formally as part of the professional recognition program.

Making decisions

Teachers want their leaders to lead. They want to know where the school is heading. They want to know the plan for success. They want you to make decisions and be decisive.

Celebrating success

Many leaders talk about celebrating success but most do not do this. Yet it is so important for staff morale. At Bellfield we regularly celebrated our successes. It started off with shared lunchtimes and afternoons at Curriculum Days. We celebrated success. It was real and not just spoken about in staff meetings. It generated a heightened staff feeling of team and individual satisfaction.

Persistence

Persistence is one of the essential ingredients for effective teachers and leaders. Persist until you get it right. Persist until the changes are embedded. Persist until the student has understood the concept or developed the skill.

Leadership talk

Talk to your staff about leadership and your perspective on leadership. Be open. Be approachable. Highlight the positive aspects of the job.

Curriculum knowledge

It is important for our school leaders to have a very sound grounding in curriculum knowledge and content. Be the curriculum leader in the school. Do not delegate this crucial task. It is central to school improvement.

Consistency

It is very important for school leaders to be consistent. Have a set of school plans and stick to them. Do not take on every new initiative or your staff will sink in change. The Four Pillars controlled our curriculum. If a new initiative fitted with the Pillars, then we would consider it. If it did not, then it was not discussed. The Four Pillars, the Three Imperatives and the smaller goals that flowed from these were all consistent year after year. The message remained the same. Of course, continual improvement was built in and constant refinement expected.

Involvement

Be involved in school activities. At Bellfield I was involved in all sport seasons as a coach and I was the School Camps Coordinator. I regularly attended excursions and regularly visited classrooms. I had an active involvement with the students.

Effective leadership is quite obviously an important ingredient in school professional learning and development cultures in schools. Strategic planning is also essential in developing a professional learning and development culture. A leader needs to know where she or he is heading. Leaders need to manage change but if goals are clear and achievable then the task is made easier. Principals must be the curriculum leader. They must establish effective means to build teacher capacity in an ongoing manner. This will then lead to continuous student improvement in academic performance. It will also support value adding. This, I believe, will be a concept that gains more and more credibility. I am sure that in the future education systems will find ways to measure value adding. This will then give a true indication of school and teacher performance.

Haileybury 2006

I took up my position as Head of Precinct of Haileybury College, Berwick, in 2006. The site is known as Edrington. There are three other campuses at Brighton (Castlefield) and Keysborough (Newlands and Senior School).

Edrington, Castlefield and Newlands have Early Learning Centres, which include Reception (3-year-olds) and Pre-Prep (4-year-olds), and Junior schools, which comprise Prep to Year 4. The Middle School covers Years 5 to 8. This is where the parallel education structure is implemented. There are both girls' and boys' Middle schools in separate areas of Haileybury. The students in Years 5–8 study the core curriculum, especially literacy and numeracy, in single-gender classrooms. This is based on strong research indicating that from this age boys learn better in all-boy classes and girls learn better in all-girl classes. This structure is maintained in Pre-Senior (Year 9) and then into Senior School (Years 10, 11 and 12). Each section of the school has a Head of School.

The entire school has around 2700 students; Edrington ELC to Year 9 has just under 600 students.

The culture at Edrington is in stark contrast to what I first found at Bellfield. The relationships between staff and students are strong. The students are well behaved, have a strong sense of values and work hard at school. The students generally achieve well above statewide benchmarks at all year levels across all campuses.

The school is fiercely committed to continuous improvement and I was clearly set the goal of implementing a process to achieve even higher academic performance from Early Learning Centre through to Year 8. At my first Edrington Executive Meeting the process was set in place (see Figure 7).

As Haileybury is a much larger school than Bellfield, many of the strategies I used at Bellfield will need to be adapted. Due to the size of

---

Edrington Executive Meeting 19/1/2006

Agenda

1 Welcome
2 Loyalty
3 John's role—curriculum leadership/classroom visits
4 Leadership Team expectations
5 Building Leadership Capacity
6 Continuous Improvement/Core business = student performance
7 Monday PD
8 Area Meetings—Givens
9 Meeting Schedules
10 General Business

Figure 7   Emphasising continual improvement, Haileybury College

the school, the heads of school will have to take on many of the roles I fulfilled at Bellfield. They will need to conduct the classroom visits and the interview system. They will need to be curriculum leaders. It is interesting because this was a question I was often asked at Bellfield: how would you implement your strategies at a much larger school?

Like all schools, the challenge for Haileybury at Edrington is to establish a professional learning and performance culture at the campus and to generate continuous school improvement in terms of student achievement.

8

Postscript

In 2006 I was able to visit and evaluate the Success For All and Challenger School Programs in the United States. I spent two weeks visiting schools in Nevada and California. I visited four Challenger schools, Lone Mountain and Silverado in Las Vegas and Almaden and Shawnee in San Jose, and Merlinda Elementary and Salvador Elementary schools in Los Angeles and Napa.

Merlinda Elementary School and Salvador Elementary School were government schools recommended to me by Robert Slavin himself as two of the very best examples of Success for All schools in the United States. Both have won several significant awards for their success with literacy instruction.

I had read a great deal about the Success for All Literacy program. It had been researched by six different US universities and they all reached the same conclusion: the program supports significant improvement in student literacy achievement levels.

The Challenger schools first came to my attention via a former Bellfield teaching colleague who had actually taught at Lone Mountain for two years. She had been exceptionally impressed with their teaching philosophy and incredibly high expectations and academic standards. There are twenty-three Challenger schools. They are currently all in the western half of the United States. They are rapidly expanding and are high-fee-paying private schools. They receive no government funding. The average Challenger student is at the 90th percentile in national testing.

In developing my thoughts surrounding highly effective schools, I have found that there are three essential components:

1 belief—belief by the staff that all students can be high performers.
2 curriculum delivery—effective curriculum delivery that focuses on the four pillars: teacher-accountable learning, explicit instruction,

moving student knowledge from short-term to long-term memory and effective relationships between students and teachers.

3   culture—the practices within the school that enhance the climate and tone: clear teacher and student commitment to expectations of high academic performance; emphasis on uniform/dress code; high standards of student behaviour, student movement, class tone and student values.

The three components of highly effective schools were certainly clearly evident at all the schools I visited in the United States. Furthermore, the effective strategies used at Bellfield were also on display in these schools, confirming in mind these strategies as excellent practice.

I would highlight the following points on the importance of an effective professional learning environment and as the essential ingredients of a high-performing school with practices guided by evidence-based research:

1   A particularly strong emphasis on the use of student achievement data to guide evaluations and assessment of curriculum programs.

2   The delivery of curriculum was structured, sequential, explicit and skills based.

3   The emphasis on letter/sound relationships instruction through the development of phonemic awareness and phonic skills.

4   The rejection of immersion-based strategies where students learnt at their own pace.

5   The setting of minimum and rigorous benchmarks for all students.

6   Strong accountability measures in terms of teacher performance and student achievement.

7   High expectations of student performance.

8   Professional development and staff appraisal clearly linked to student performance outcomes.

9   Application of Direct Instruction teaching and learning principles.

10   The intensity in which teachers delivered the curriculum.

Appendix 1: Teacher excellence

In 2000 I developed a Teacher Excellence document. This was used as a guide by many teachers, especially the younger ones, in improving their teacher practice.

Teacher Excellence
The two key aspects of teacher excellence are **high expectations** and **student accountability**. Excellent teachers present curriculum content to children that they **retain** and **can use effectively**.
Children develop a **pride** in their work. Children are **highly motivated** and are **actively engaged** in their learning.
It is demonstrated by:

Presentation Skills
Children display neat and attractive handwriting. Correct letter formation is actively taught. Work is neatly set out with no scribbling.

Automatic Response
Children are motivated to learn the age-appropriate automatic-response number skills and retain them.

Mathematics
Children have a thorough knowledge and understanding of the key mathematical concepts.

English
Children develop effective letter/sound knowledge that they can use effectively in reading and writing (spelling).
Sentence construction and formation is effectively modelled and applied.
Children use correct, age-appropriate grammar and punctuation.
Creativity and imagination are enhanced.
Children learn that there is a structure to effective writing.
Children learn to express themselves effectively.

Studies of Society and Environment
Children learn to form opinions and make judgements that they can reasonably validate and support via Inquiry Learning.

Children develop a wide general knowledge.
Children develop appropriate social skills.

Science
Children learn to hypothesise and to test to explain physical phenomena.

Control
Children behave appropriately.

Resiliency
The teacher acts as an effective role model developing children's self worth and setting appropriate goals.

Climate
The classroom has a friendly and caring environment with an emphasis on motivation to learn.

Support
The teacher displays active support for their team and the leadership.

Canter
The teacher agrees with Canter's notion of developing effective relationships with all students.

Values
The teacher effectively engenders the school's Code of Conduct values.

Planning
Planning is always thorough and well informed.

Preparation
Classroom preparation is seen to be of the highest standard.

Correction
All student work is corrected or at least acknowledged where appropriate.

Assessment and Reporting/Recordkeeping
Thorough, accurate and effectively utilised.

Display
Classroom display is of the highest standard.

Parent Communication
Friendly and effective.

Professional Development
The teacher always keeps abreast of school Professional Development and actively engages in implementing this in the classroom.

THE ULTIMATE MEASURE OF TEACHER EFFECTIVENESS IS HOW FAR INDIVIDUAL CHILDREN WITHIN A CLASSROOM GO TOWARDS REACHING THEIR FULL ACADEMIC POTENTIAL.

Appendix 2: Induction program timetable

Term 1	
Wednesday, 25 January	Overview • Curriculum • Professional responsibilities • Planning • Control • Professional growth Expectations—Students • Pupil movement • Bookwork/ Presentation • Work completion • Tone • Work routines • Correction • Roving eye • Lining up Expectations—Teachers • Punctuality • Effective planning • Team • Display • Work Program Probation/Annual Performance Review • Professional Standards • Bellfield's Program • Individual Professional Development Plans
Wednesday, 17 February	General Questions • Issues raised by Inductees • Control • Work routines • Assessment/Evaluation

Wednesday, 17 February (*continued*)	<ul><li>Early Years Literacy</li><li>Numeracy Strategies</li><li>Administration—rolls, cash receipts, etc.</li><li>Student Support Group</li><li>Parent–Teacher Interviews</li></ul>
Wednesday, 15 March	General Questions<ul><li>Issues raised by Inductees</li><li>Homework</li><li>Work completion</li><li>Expectations</li><li>Bookwork/Presentation</li><li>Children with Special Needs</li><li>Developing connections—rapport</li><li>Display</li><li>Planning—individual/team</li><li>Dealing with parents</li></ul>
Term 2	
Wednesday, 26 May	School Charter Code of Conduct Child Management June Reports June Evaluation Parent–Teacher Interviews Questions/other issues
Wednesday, 2 June	Numeracy Issues Professional Development Team Questions/other issues
Wednesday, 9 June	Literacy SOSE Staff Welfare Annual Performance Review—Mid-cycle interviews Questions/other issues
Term 3	
Wednesday, 14 July	Phonemic Awareness—Dr John Munro Staff Professional Development Bellfield Phonemic Awareness Program Teaching strategies Effective implementation/planning Children experiencing difficulties

Wednesday, 11 August	Effective use of flashcards Numeracy—daily routines for counting/tables etc. Spelling Writing Handwriting Questions/other issues
Wednesday, 1 September	Review • General review of all matters covered so far this year. • There will be a particular emphasis on ENJOYMENT of the teaching role and the SATISFYING aspects of the job. • MAKING CONNECTIONS with children and techniques for developing their SELF-ESTEEM • Reflection on the need for constant EVALUATION of teaching performance in terms of planning and the implementation of EFFECTIVE teaching and learning strategies.
Term 4	
Wednesday, 6 October	Phonemic Awareness • Dr John Munro will be present to design a Professional Development Program to suit the needs of our Inductees. This will follow a similar format to that undertaken by all class teachers in 1998. This will include John in several classroom visits followed by debriefing sessions with each teacher.
Wednesday, 20 October	Applying for vacancies • Overall process • Advertisements • Job Description and Selection Criteria • Written Application • Selection Process—short-listing • Interviews • Thorough examination of the issues surrounding applying for and preparing for job vacancies.

Wednesday, 17 November	General review of the 1999 induction process
	• Evaluation
	• Recommendations for improvement
	Career structure
	• Skills
	• Records
	• Mentors

Appendix 3: Professional development strategy

Professional Development Strategy

Coordinator

John Fleming is the Professional Development Coordinator. However, other members of the School Leadership Team comprising Assistant Principal/Senior School Coordinator and Leading Teacher/Junior School Coordinator will be responsible for the organisation of all Professional Development and the implementation of this strategy.

Decision-Making Process and Timeline

- In Term 1 all staff will be informed of the Teacher/Staff Personal Professional Development Strategy, Proformas and Priorities.
- Interviews will be conducted late Term 1 with all teaching and ancillary staff. These interviews will be conducted by the Principal after seeking feedback from Area Coordinators.
- The following steps have been identified:
  - Personal Professional Development Planning discussed at Staff Meeting.
  - At Area Meetings Personal Professional Development Proformas, Professional Development Strategy and Professional Development Priorities discussed.
  - At Ancillary Staff Meeting the Personal Professional Development Proformas, Strategy and Priorities will be discussed.
- Interviews will be conducted during the last weeks of Term 1.
- Staff feedback and agreement at our Staff Meeting and Ancillary Staff Meeting regarding this Strategy, Proformas and Priorities.
- Proformas distributed mid-term.
- A Whole School Professional Development Plan will be compiled mid-Term 1. This will incorporate aspects of our Whole School Professional Development Priorities as well as Personal Professional Development Priorities.
- Term 3—Review of Whole School Plan and Priorities as part of our Program Plans and Budgets process.
- Feedback obtained via the Annual Report Staff Survey.

- The Plans will be of one year's duration.
- Identified needs will be prioritised by the Leadership Team.
- Money will be allocated to staff according to specified needs.
- We hope all wants will be addressed but, if they cannot be, the Leadership Team will determine a priority list for the allocation of monies.
- The Leadership Team will integrate the Individual Plans with the Whole School Plan.

Appendix 4: Annual professional development plan

The annual professional development plan described the process for determining Professional Development activities for the year. It was always aligned with our School Charter goals and key learning area recommendations. Professional development was ongoing and consistent. It always focused on classroom practice. The performance review process was used to ensure that teachers were implementing the strategies and refining their own performance.

(The development agenda was made up of our key curriculum area recommendations, developed each year. These recommendations specifically guided improvement in our teaching and learning programs.)

Annual Professional Development Plan

The Bellfield Primary School Professional Development Plan consists of the following components:

A: Whole School Priorities
Our Whole School Professional Development Priorities are determined each year during our Annual Program Plans and Budgets processes. They form part of an ongoing Five Year Plan. The priorities take into account our School Charter needs as an integral component of our Five Year Cycle.

- Literacy including Reading Recovery
- Numeracy
- Triennial Review
- New School Charter
- SOSE
- Learning Technologies
- Code of Conduct—reviewing and developing a new Policy
- Developing new Policies in the Arts and LOTE
- Early Years of Schooling Conference

Key Priorities
1 Implementation of new Charter Goals and Priorities
2 Mathematics P–6 Number Program Implementation and development of appropriate assessment practices

---

3   English
4   Code of Conduct
5   Learning Technologies implemented into classroom programs
6   Writing P–6
7   Development of children's application and thinking skills across all Key Learning Areas
8   Assessment and Reporting Policy

B: Priorities developed through our Personal Professional Development Strategy

The identification of Whole School Priorities will form a significant component of Staff Personal Professional Development Plans. These priorities will be addressed through the Professional Development Plan Timelines established for Terms 2, 3 and 4. All staff will include Learning Technologies as an Area for Development within their Personal Professional Development Plans. Support will be provided by the Coordinator, the Learning Technologies Committee and via DE&T publications.

C: Activities

- Staff Meetings—Term PD Plans
- Planning Days
- Classroom visits
- Mentoring/Coaching
- Area Meetings
- Team Planning:
  - resources
  - teaching strategies
  - evaluation/assessment
  - integrated curriculum
  - Unit Planners
  - student achievement levels
- School visits
- Networks—Transition, Principal, Assistant Principal, etc
- Curriculum Days
- Professional reading
- Conferences/Seminars
- Professional Associations—ACHPER, STAV, MAV, etc
- Peer support
- In-service activities

Appendix 5: Key curriculum area recommendations (2005)

Key Curriculum Area Recommendations 2005

Major recommendations
CONTINUE TEACHER MENTORING PROGRAM
DISPLAY—classroom/corridor
Emphasis on our Four Pillars
All children to effectively learn tables and automatic response-letters home, assemblies, awards, House competition
Written Expression/Proofreading
Challenge our more capable students
Handwriting
Thinking curriculum—further incorporate John Munro's strategies

Overall
- Ensure all work is corrected.
- Ensure all work is neat and tidy—no scribbles, no cross-outs, no spaces
- Further develop excellent handwriting and presentation skills in all students with a significant emphasis in Term 1
- Revision Week—start of each Term
- Continue refinement of literacy strategies
- Continue refinement of numeracy strategies
- Intervention Programs P–6 to continue
- Friday Book to continue in Junior School to review spelling, dictation and number. Emphasis on writing more effective and interesting sentences.
- Effectively implement Student Welfare Programs
- Emphasis on lining up and movement around school
- Strategies for latecomers to continue to be monitored
- Announcements over PA to be kept to a minimum and the intercom used where possible
- Individual Learning Plans to be developed for specific children
- **Further develop effective strategies for enhancing our students' abilities to perform well in test situations**
- **Healthy Snack Days**

- **Implement Kids'n'Fruit Program**
- **Junior/Senior School Assemblies**

English
- Professional Development in reading comprehension
- Further refine Whole School Grammar Planner
- Purchase phonic resource books
- Monitor the use of the Lexiles Program
- Teacher directed Reading to continue P–6 with refinements to improve the program regularly considered
- Focus on cloze, correct answers, fill-the-gap comprehension, multiple-choice skills and RPT strategies
- Regular weekly spelling testing for all children Grades 1–6 with spelling lists going home on a weekly basis
- **Ensure children produce the relevant quality and number of written pieces as stated in our Policy and emphasise the creative aspect of writing**
- Emphasis on narrative
- **Emphasis on proofreading**
- Continue implementation and refinement of Fitzroy Readers
- Continue implementation of SRA Readers
- **Ensure quiet movement between groups during literacy sessions**
- Implement effective teaching strategies that develop thinking, understanding and analytical abilities in line with the John Munro PD
- Cater for the specific needs of NESB children
- Continue the very successful assessment and evaluation program already established
- Continue to timetable Literacy sessions in blocks P–6
- **Renewed emphasis on Speaking and Listening to include formal presentations**
- **Emphasis on vocabulary extension and understanding—word knowledge**

Mathematics—Number
- Continue to prioritise Mathematics timetabling with an emphasis on larger blocks of time
- Audit Mathematics equipment
- Continue to consolidate Mathematics Term Planners, Assessment Procedures and Program Content P–6
- Plan blocks of lessons in the Junior School with Friday being Revision Day and to maintain the double blocks
- Plan blocks of lessons on topics in the Senior School with regular revision
- Investigate ways of extending those children who have the ability to make mental computations and have a solid understanding of Mathematics

- **Ensure all children P–6 learn their Mental computations i.e. tables and number facts by exploring further strategies to improve these skills. Children to be made accountable through regular testing**
- Effective use of diagnostic tests and the NT
- Test children on a regular basis
- **Follow up on Place Value PD and implement for all Strands**

Mathematics—Measurement
- Determine the most effective way of timetabling Measurement Mathematics in both Junior and Senior Schools
- Use of Buddy Time where relevant for Applied Mathematics

Appendix 6: Performance and development culture questionnaire report (April 2005)

Performance and Development Culture Questionnaire Report April 2005

Customised Individual Teacher Development Plans—overall score 4.7
My plan is aligned with what I really need if I am to increase my
    effectiveness 4.9
My plan is aligned with the school's priorities for improvement 4.8
My school ensures my plan is up to date 4.7
My school has assisted me in developing my plan 4.5
My school has supported the implementation of my plan 4.7
My professional learning in this school has had a positive effect on my
    career prospects 4.7

Quality Professional Development—overall score 4.8
I have increased knowledge of strategies for teaching content 4.8
I have increased understanding of differences among students and how
    to cater for them 4.9
I have increased understanding of linking assessment to the teaching
    and learning cycle 4.7
I make clearer links between teaching goals and classroom
    activities 4.7
I now manage classroom activities and transitions more effectively 4.8
I now use more effective teaching and learning strategies appropriate to
    my students 4.8
I integrate assessment and teaching and learning more effectively 4.9
I provide more effective feedback to my students to support
    their learning 4.9
I access and use materials and resources more effectively 4.8
My students are learning more purposefully 4.8
My students are more actively engaged in learning activities 4.9
My confidence as a teacher has increased 4.8

Performance and Development Culture—overall score 4.9
My job provides me with professional stimulation and growth 4.7
I have many opportunities to learn new things in this school 4.7

I feel supported in my teaching   4.9
I have a sense that education in this school is improving   5.0
My abilities are recognised and used effectively   4.8
I have a sense of continuing professional development   4.8
I am feeling increasingly effective   4.7
I get good advice from other teachers in this school   4.9
In this school, teachers are recognised for a job well done   4.9
I feel supported by the school leadership team to try out new ideas   4.7
The principal knows and communicates what kind of school he or
   she wants   5.0
The teachers who teach well in this school are given leadership
   opportunities   4.9
Teachers maintain high standards in their teaching   5.0
In this school, we solve problems; we don't just talk about them   4.9
Teachers regularly evaluate how well programs meet students'
   needs   4.9
There is cooperation among teachers to provide quality learning
   opportunities   4.8
Joint review of students' progress is a normal part of the way
   we work   4.9
Most teachers in this school are willing to share teaching practices
   and ideas   5.0
Teachers in this school keep abreast of recent research   4.8
Most teachers think that students in this school are capable of
   learning   5.0
The school leadership team knows the teachers who are most
   effective   4.9
The school leadership team expects teachers to be accountable   4.9
The school leadership team values the knowledge and skills of
   teachers   4.9
The school leadership team provides opportunities for teachers to give
   feedback   4.9
The school leadership team is responsive to staff suggestions for
   change   4.9
The school leadership team is concerned to create an effective work
   environment   5.0
The school leadership team provides opportunities to gain leadership
   experience   4.7
The school leadership team promotes collaboration and reflection   4.9

Appendix 7: Teacher performance and appraisal 2006

Edrington

Teacher Performance and Appraisal 2006
1   PRP Interview
2   Classroom visits
3   Interview/feedback
4   Formal documentation
5   PD/Mentoring

Aims
1   To improve teacher practice, i.e. to build teacher capacity.
2   To enhance teacher career and leadership skills.
3   To support curriculum development at the school.

Classroom Visits Check List
- Display
- Presentation
- Time on task
- Organisation
- Tone
- Student management
- Planning
- Lesson structure
- Questioning
- Use of resources
- Student feedback
- Student engagement
- Work routines
- Clarity of instructions
- Correction
- Expectations

References

Achinstein, B 2002, 'Conflict amid community: The micropolitics of teacher collaboration', *Teachers College Record*, vol. 4, no. 3, pp. 421–55.

Australian Science Teachers Association 2002, *Professional standards for highly accomplished teachers of science*, Australian Science Teachers Association, Canberra.

Boston Consulting Group 2003, *Schools workforce development strategy*, Victorian Department of Education and Training, Melbourne.

Brophy, J (ed.) 1991, *Teacher's knowledge of subject matter as it relates to their teaching practice*, vol. 2, JAI Press Inc., London.

Canady, RL, & Rettig, MD 1995, *Block scheduling: A catalyst for change in high schools*, Eye on Education, Princeton, New Jersey.

Copland, M 2001, 'The myth of the superprincipal', *Phi Delta Kappan*, vol. 82, no. 7, pp. 528–33.

Cranston, N, Tromans, C, & Reugebrink, M 2004, 'Forgotten leaders: What do we know about the deputy principalship in secondary schools?', *International Journal of Leadership in Education*, vol. 7, no. 3, pp. 225–42.

Cushman, K 1989, 'Schedules that bind', *American Educator*, vol. 13, no. 2, pp. 35–9.

Darling-Hammond, L 1988, 'Accountability and teacher professionalism', *American Educator*, vol. 12, no. 4, Winter, pp. 8–13, 38–43.

—— & Sykes, G (eds) 1999, *Teaching as the learning profession: Handbook of policy and practice*, Jossey-Bass, San Francisco.

Day, C, & Harris, A 2002, 'Teacher leadership, reflective practice, and school improvement', in K Leithwood & P Hallinger (eds), *Second international handbook of educational leadership and administration*, Part 2, pp. 957–77, Kluwer, Dordrecht.

Drago-Severson, E 2004, *Helping teachers learn: Principal leadership for adult growth and development*, Corwin Press, Thousand Oaks, California.

Finley, MK 1984, 'Teachers and tracking in a comprehensive high school', *Sociology of Education*, vol. 57, no. 4, pp. 233–43.

Fullan, M 1982, *The meaning of educational change*, Teachers College Press, New York.

—— 2001, *Leading in a culture of change*, Jossey-Bass, San Francisco.

—— & Hargreaves, A 1991, *What's worth fighting for? Working together for your school*, Regional Laboratory for Educational Improvement, Andover, Massachusetts.

Garet, MS, Porter, AC, Desimone, L, Birman, BF, & Yoon, KS 2001, 'What makes professional development effective? Results from a national sample of teachers', *American Educational Research Journal*, vol. 38, pp. 915–45.

Gehrke, N, & Sheffield, R 1985, 'Career mobility of women and minority high school teachers during decline', *Journal of Research and Development in Education*, vol. 18, no. 4, pp. 39–49.

Grace, G 1995, *School leadership: Beyond education management—an essay in policy scholarship*, Falmer, London.

Gronn, P 2004, 'Distribution of leadership', in GR Goethals, GJ Sorenson & J MacGregor Burns (eds), *Encyclopaedia of Leadership*, vol. 1., Sage, Thousand Oaks, California.

Grossman, P, Wineburg, S, & Woolworth, S 2001, 'Toward a theory of teacher community', *Teachers College Record*, vol. 103, no. 6, pp. 942–1012.

Gutiérrez, R 1996, 'Practices, beliefs, and cultures of high school mathematics departments: Understanding their influences on student advancement', *Journal of Curriculum Studies*, vol. 28, no. 5, pp. 495–530.

Hargreaves, A, & Fullan, M, 1998, *What's worth fighting for out there?*, Australian Council for Educational Administration inc (ACEA) association with the Ontario Public School Teachers Federation, Sydney.

Hargreaves, DH 1995, 'School culture, school effectiveness and school improvement', in BPM Greemers & D Reynold (eds), *School Effectiveness and School Improvement*, pp. 23–46, Swet, Netherlands.

Hawley, W, & Valli, L 1999, 'The essentials of effective professional development: a new consensus', in L Darling-Hammond & G Sykes (eds), *Teaching as the learning profession. Handbook of Policy and Practice*, Jossey-Bass, San Francisco.

Hill, PW, & Rowe, KJ 1995, 'Use of multi-level modeling in procedures for maximizing between-school comparability of final year school-based assessments', *Multilevel Modeling Newsletter*, vol. 7, no. 1, pp. 12–16.

Ingvarson, L 2001, 'Strengthening the profession? A comparison of recent reforms in the UK and the USA', paper presented at the International Study Association on Teachers and Teaching (ISATT), Faro, Portugal, 21–25 September.

Isaacson, N, & Bamburg, J 1992, 'Can schools become learning organizations?', *Educational Leadership*, vol. 50, no. 3, pp. 42–4.

Kennedy, K 1999, 'Constructing the teaching profession for the new millennium', *Unicorn: Journal of the Australian College of Education*, vol. 25, no. 2, pp. 3–4.

Kleinhenz, E, & Ingvarson, LC 2004, 'Teacher accountability in Australia: Current policies and practices and their relation to the improvement of teaching and learning', *Research Papers in Education*, vol. 19, no. 1.

Kruse, SD 1997, 'Reflective activity in practice: Vignettes of teachers' deliberative work', *Journal of Research and Development in Education*, vol. 31, no. 1, pp. 46–60.

Little, JW 1990, 'The persistence of privacy: Autonomy and initiative in teachers' professional relations', *Teachers College Record*, vol. 91, no. 4, pp. 509–36.

Lortie, DC 1975, *Schoolteacher: A sociological study*, University of Chicago Press, Chicago.

Louis, KS, & Kruse, SD 1995, *Professionalism and community: Perspectives on reforming urban schools*, Corwin Press, Thousand Oaks, California.

McAnninch, A 1993, *Teacher thinking and the case method: Theory and future directions*, Teachers College Press, New York and London.

McArthur, T (ed.) 1992, *The Oxford Companion to the English Language*, Oxford University Press, New York.

McLaughlin, M, & Talbert, J 2001, *Professional communities and the work of high school teaching*, University of Chicago Press, Chicago.

McLaughlin, MW, & Pfiefer, RS 1988, *Teacher evaluation. Improvement, accountability and effective learning*, Teachers College Press, New York.

McRae, D, Ainsworth, G, Groves, R, Rowland, M, & Zbar, V 2001. *PD 2000—Australia: A national mapping of school teacher professional development*, Commonwealth Department of Education, Training and Youth Affairs, Canberra.

Masters, GN 2005, 'What outcomes do we want?', *ACER eNews*, no. 34, 20 October, ACER, viewed 2006, <http://www.acer.edu.au/enews/0510_outcomes.html>.

Ministerial Council for Education, Employment, Training and Youth Affairs (MCEETYA) 2003, *A national framework for professional standards of teaching*. Ministerial Council for Education, Employment, Training and Youth Affairs, Carlton.

Mulford, B 2003, *The role of school leadership in attracting and retaining teachers and promoting innovative schools and students—Review of teaching and teacher education* Commonwealth Department of Education, Science and Training, Canberra.

Munro, J 2001, 'School Wide Literacy Improvement', *Melbourne Education*, no. 4, Autumn, p. 6.

Murphy, J, & Shipman, NJ 2003, 'Developing standards for school leadership development', in P Hallinger (ed.), *Reshaping the landscape of school leadership development: A global perspective*, Swets & Zeitlinger BV, Lisse, The Netherlands, pp. 69–84.

Neufeld, V 1984, 'Education for capability: an example of curriculum change from medical education', *Programmed Learning and Education Technology*, vol. 21, pp. 262–7.

Peterson, P, McCarthey, S, & Elmore, R 1996, 'Learning from school restructuring', *American Educational Research Journal*, vol. 33, no. 1, pp. 119–53.

Raudenbush, SW, Rowan, B, & Cheong, YF 1992, 'Contextual effects on the self-perceived efficacy of high school teachers', *Sociology of Education*, vol. 65, pp. 150–67.

Raywid, MA 1995, *The subschools/small schools movement—taking stock*, Center on Organization and Restructuring of Schools, Madison, Wisconsin.

Richardson, V (ed.) 2001, *Handbook of research on teaching*, 4th edn, American Educational Research Association, Washington.

Rozenholtz, SJ 1989, *Teachers' workplace: The social organisation of schools*, Longman, White Plains, New York.

Schein, EH 1985, *Organizational culture and leadership: A dynamic view*, Jossey-Bass, San Francisco.

Schon, D 1987, *Educating the reflective practitioner*, Jossey-Bass, San Francisco.

Senge, P 1990, *The fifth discipline: The art and practice of the learning organization*, Doubleday, New York.

Shulman, LS 1987, 'Knowledge and reaching: Foundations for the new reform', *Harvard Educational Review*, vol. 57, no. 1, pp. 1–22.

Slavin, Robert E, Madden, Nancy A, Dolan, Lawrence J, Wasik, Barbara A, 1996, *Every child, every school success for all*, Corwin Press, Thousand Oaks, California.

Stokes, L 2001, 'Lessons from an inquiring school: Forms of inquiry and conditions for teacher learning', in A Lieberman & L Miller (eds), *Teachers caught in the action: Professional development that matters*, Teachers College Press, New York.

Stoll, L 2003, 'School culture and improvement', in Preedy, M, Glatter, R, & Wise, C (eds), *Strategic leadership and educational improvement*, Paul Chapman Publishing, London.

Talbert, J 1995, 'Boundaries of teachers' professional communities in US high schools. Power and precariousness of the subject department', in L Siskin & J Little (eds), *The subjects in question. Departmental organization and the high school*, Teachers' College Press, New York.

Talbert, JE 1990, *Teacher tracking: Exacerbating inequalities in the high school*, Center for Research on the Context of Secondary Teaching, Stanford University, Stanford.

Victorian Department of Education and Early Childhood Development 2006, 'Resources – The five elements', 21 July, viewed 2007, <http://www.education.vic.gov.au/management/schoolimprovement/panddc/resources/resourcesbyelement.htm>

Victorian Department of Education and Training 2004, *The privilege and the price: A study of principal class workload and its impact on health and wellbeing*, Department of Education and Training, Melbourne.